Caring for Kangaroos and Wallabies

Dear Reader,

Enjoy our book on Kangas

Cheers, Anne W
2016

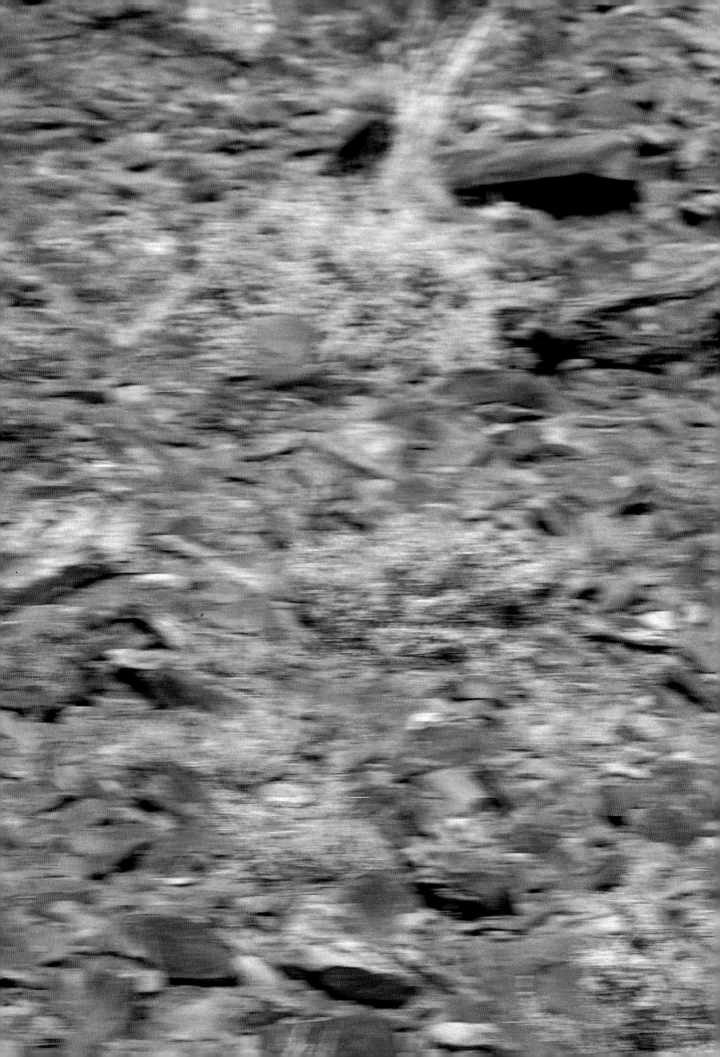

Caring for Kangaroos and Wallabies

Anne and Ray Williams

Kangaroo Press

For my mum and all loving mums,
for the love and care
they lavish on their offspring and their foster-young

CARING FOR KANGAROOS AND WALLABIES

First published in Australia in 1999 by Kangaroo Press
an imprint of Simon & Schuster (Australia) Pty Limited
20 Barcoo Street, East Roseville NSW 2069

A Viacom Company
Sydney New York London Toronto Tokyo Singapore

National Library of Australia
Cataloguing-in-Publication data

Williams, Anne, 1952–
Caring for Kangaroos and Wallabies.
Bibliography.
Includes index.

ISBN 0 86417 897 2

1. Kangaroos - Australia - Handling. 2. Wallabies - Australia -
Handling. I. Williams, Ray, 1946– . II. Title.

599.220994

Maps by Margaret Hastie

Set in Times 10/13
Printed in Hong Kong by Colorcraft Ltd

10 9 8 7 6 5 4 3 2 1

Contents

List of Tables

Amy & Tanya with Swamp Wallaby and Wallaroo joeys on their laps

Foreword

Kangaroos are the largest of the living marsupials, and perhaps the most familiar icon of Australia. Yet few people appreciate the unusual biology or extraordinary diversity of kangaroos, and even fewer have the privilege of living with and observing the animals at close quarters.

The authors of this book, Anne, with her husband Ray, have spent many years studying the habits of kangaroos in handling and caring for young animals that have been orphaned or injured. She describes where you are most likely to see the different species of kangaroos, their distinguishing features, habitats, diets and social behaviour. More importantly, she provides clear practical guidelines for fostercarers who need to know how best to look after kangaroos and how to rehabilitate them after recovery. Anne Williams brings a wealth of knowledge and personal experience to her subject, and it is a great pleasure to recommend this book to all with an interest in the care and management of some of Australia's most curious native mammals.

Chris Dickman
University of Sydney
January 1999

Acknowledgments

We would like to thank all those friends and associates with whom we have shared and swapped helpful hints and information about caring for kangaroos and wallabies over the past twenty-seven years. During this time, Ray and I have been involved with the care, study and maintenance of our Australian wildlife while fostering native wildlife, working in wildlife parks, managing the University of New South Wales Field Station near Sydney and carrying out wildlife surveys.

We would like to thank our twin daughters, Amy and Tanya, who have spent many hours of their lives, from a very young age, helping us to care for orphaned and injured wildlife. They have learnt to appreciate the needs of these creatures and the time required to help them. They also get the greatest pleasure, with us, in seeing an animal successfully released after rehabilitation to continue its natural way of life.

We thank our many friends who offered to read and comment on the text, starting with our daughter Tanya, who spent many laborious hours reading through it thoroughly, as well as Barbara Smith, Karen Carragher, Mathew Bell, Joan Hayllar, Richard Rowles and Eileen Hogbin.

Our special thanks go to Yvonne and Dennis Browning for their friendship and help over the years and for the use of many of Dennis's photos of different orphans of various ages in the section on hand-raising.

We wish to thank Ian Morris, Alex Dudley, Rob Close, Mark Eldridge, Arthur White and Sandy Ingleby for the much appreciated use of their photographs to complete the Identification section. Each photographer's name is acknowledged in the caption. Any photograph not so acknowledged has been taken by the authors.

Lastly, but not least, we thank Dr Chris Dickman, for spending his valuable time in reading this book and giving his professional opinion, and for providing us with a Foreword.

Anne and Ray Williams

PART I

INTRODUCTION TO KANGAROOS, WALLABIES & RAT-KANGAROOS

Head and shoulders of male Eastern Grey Kangaroo

What is a Macropod? What is a Marsupial? Kangaroos are Both!

Macropodoidea is the name of the superfamily encompassing kangaroos, wallabies, rat-kangaroos, tree-kangaroos and potoroos. The name is derived from two Greek words—*macro* meaning 'big' and *pod* meaning 'foot'.

Macropods are herbivorous marsupials with short forelimbs, long hindlimbs adapted for hopping (their main form of locomotion) and long muscular tails. They range in size from the largest species, the kangaroos, through the medium-sized wallabies and pademelons to the smallest species, the potoroos and rat-kangaroos.

Macropods are found in all types of habitats in Australia— deserts, rainforests, mountains and grasslands. Many species are specialised to cope with extremes in temperatures and conditions. Some now survive in very small areas of protected remnant habitats, such as the Bridled Nailtail Wallaby found only in the Brigalow Scrub near Dingo, Queensland.

Macropods are just one group among the marsupial mammals, which have a pouch or fold of skin (marsupium) on the abdomen which contains the mammary glands and in which they carry developing offspring. Marsupial young are attached to the mother by a placenta for only a very short time prior to their birth, which occurs at a very early stage of development. The embryonic young transfer to the pouch, which is like a substitute uterus, to finish their foetal development, and consequently can be said to be 'born' when they are permanently out of the pouch.

Evolutionary outline

Two families have evolved within the superfamily Macropodoidea—the Potoroidae (potoroos and rat-kangaroos) and the Macropodidae (kangaroos and wallabies). These two families are quite different in their eating habits—the Potoroidae are omnivorous, the main diet of many of them including fungi and insects, whereas the Macropodidae feed mainly on grasses, herbs, shrubs and leaves.

The ancestors of kangaroos were originally tree-dwellers which gradually evolved into ground-dwellers. As this occurred their tooth structure changed, from thin-cutting omnivorous teeth suited to dealing with worms, insects, fruit and small vertebrates (small animals and birds) to the heavily-crowned teeth seen now in Red Kangaroos, for example, which are suited to grinding tough grasses.

The earliest fossil record of kangaroo ancestors, weighing about 5 kg, dates back 25 million years. Between 15 million and 8 million years ago these ancestors began to differentiate, many growing much larger. Australia at that time was largely a rainforest environment.

About 8 million years ago the central areas of the continent began to dry out; the rainforests survived only around the edges, much as they exist today. The larger macropods, the kangaroos, were successful in adapting to these drier conditions; presumably many of the small rainforest types became extinct except in areas where the rainforest survived. By now there were many species, some weighing up to 60 kg, the size of modern day kangaroos and wallaroos. The larger of these species, in the more open habitats, appear to have developed a two-legged hopping gait, but those which lived in the denser habitats, like the rat-kangaroos that appeared by the late Miocene/early Pliocene (between 6 million and 4 million years ago), still used a bounding gait (on all four limbs). These later developed into the bettongs, potoroos and Musky Rat-kangaroos. Their tooth structure was still adapted to browsing on shrubbery, not yet to eating grass.

During the Pliocene era (5 million to 2 million years ago), much of Australia was open savannah and woodlands. The deserts had not yet appeared and the macropods of the time were similar to modern day Grey Kangaroos, rock-wallabies and pademelons. This was the period of the giant marsupials. The largest of the kangaroo types were the Grey Kangaroo's ancestors, among them the short-faced *Simosthenurus* species, which weighed up to 150 kg and persisted throughout the Pleistocene period. These early kangaroos had only one major toe on the hind foot; the third and fourth fingers of the hand were elongated, possibly used for pulling down branches to feed on leaves. The *Troposodon*, one genus that flourished through this period, were browsers which weighed between 20 and 120 kg. Most of the small species evolved during this period. As the short-faced species became dominant, the less specialised *troposodons* (about the size of wallaroos) became extinct, possibly because of competition for food and/or space.

The Pleistocene period (2 million to 10 000 years ago) brought about many environmental changes. The climate grew alternately cooler and warmer several times—the ice at the poles grew and then melted, altering the sea levels each time. This is when many animals moved between islands and the mainland as the landmasses were joined and separated repeatedly. At the conclusion of the ice age, groups of fauna became isolated and evolved into new species. As ice developed at the poles, rainfall and temperatures dropped and Australia's centre became covered in sand dunes as the winds eroded surfaces where little vegetation now grew. The highest mountains became snow-covered and the rainforests shrank even more.

Macropods suited to the more arid conditions now evolved, like the Desert Rat-kangaroo (*Caloprymnus campestris*) and the Red Kangaroo (*Macropus rufus*). Fossils of these species appear in the Pleistocene period, along with the remains of giant kangaroos that could have weighed as much as 200–300 kg. One of these giant kangaroos was *Procoptodon goliah,* whose fossil remains have been found in the Menindee area in western New South Wales and elsewhere in Australia. Also around at the time was *Propleopus*, a rat-kangaroo which weighed over 70 kg and appears from its tooth structure to have been carnivorous (meat/insect eating). Some other fossil remains from 2 million years ago have green-coloured remains in their stomach areas and invaluable impressions of fur, nails and skin. Even more spectacularly, on rare occasions the remains of pouch young have been found.

Between 20 000 and 10 000 years ago, many of the very large animals became extinct. The largest remaining kangaroo was the Red Kangaroo, which as we know it now can reach a weight of 90 kg. Some of the smaller macropods also became extinct, while others simply shrank in size. Just why Eastern and Western Grey Kangaroos and Agile Wallabies shrank, or why others disappeared, is uncertain, but two theories are currently being debated. Humans arrived in Australia at least 60 000 years ago, about the time that the extinctions occurred. Quite a bit of evidence points to Pleistocene man hunting the large mammals to extinction. On the other continents, Europe and North and South America, many larger animals disappeared at this time under similar circumstances. The other theory suggests that climatic changes caused the disappearances.

More recently, from 10 000 to 200 years ago, little has changed in the evolution of the macropods. Since European settlement, six species have been lost—the Toolache Wallaby, the Eastern Hare-wallaby, the Central Hare-wallaby, the Crescent Nailtail Wallaby, the Broad-faced Potoroo and the Desert Rat-kangaroo. In addition, the ranges of the Rufous Hare-wallaby, the Banded Hare-wallaby and the Bridled Nailtail Wallaby have diminished to less than 5 per cent of their previous distribution.

Remnants of meat/insect-eating habits still exist among some macropods—we have witnessed pademelons eating millipedes and the Allied Rock-wallaby has been filmed eating caterpillars. Many wallabies in particular, and some of the larger kangaroos, will quite readily nibble on cooked chicken, bacon and dog biscuits.

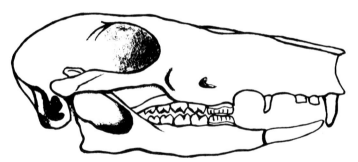

The skull of a potoroo shows the canines and the pointed incisors, plus the long cutting premolars adapted to eating an insectivorous diet (Tanya Williams)

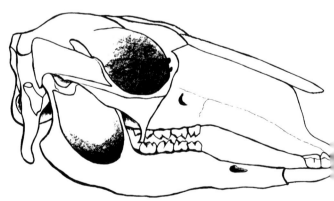

The Red Kangaroo skull shows the heavier molars used for grinding vegetation; no canines are present between incisors and molars (Tanya Williams)

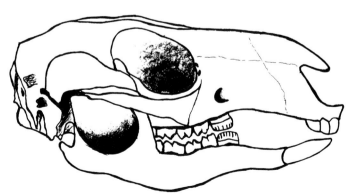

Swamp Wallaby skull showing the broad premolars that both Swamp Wallabies and Agile Wallabies never shed (Tanya Williams)

◄ 2 ►

Species of Macropods

In this chapter we just touch on general information about each species. More detailed information can be sought in the references given on pages 106–8. Identification photographs appear with location maps in Chapter 4.

It is not often recognised just how many species there are in the kangaroo families. The large animals such as the Red and Grey Kangaroos and some of the wallabies are most commonly seen, and are well known, but there are many which live fairly secretive, nocturnal lives and are rarely seen by the general public.

After the Latin name of each species we provide an interpretation of how the species names were originally derived (after Strahan 1981, 1995). Many of them are descriptive of colouration or a defining physical feature, e.g. 'long-nose'.

Potoroos and Musky Rat-kangaroo

Long-nosed Potoroo (*Potorous tridactylus*) [*Potorous* = Aboriginal word for potoroo, *tridactylus* = 'three-toed'] The early explorers thought that the animal's double grooming claw was only one toe. These potoroos live in areas of coastal heath and wet and dry sclerophyll forests in south-eastern Australia and Tasmania. They favour thick groundcover out of which they rarely venture, as they then become vulnerable to predators. The potoroos move about under cover of shrubbery, digging for fungi (over 50 species are eaten) and grubs, insects, insect larvae, tubers and roots in light sandy soils. Illustrated on page 45.

Long-footed Potoroo (*Potorous longipes*) [*longipes* = 'long-footed'] This potoroo has a similar diet to its relative but may live in slightly more open forest with a dense understorey on friable clayey soils. It is 50 per cent larger and heavier than the Long-nosed Potoroo and more robust. It was only recently rediscovered in the eastern Gippsland area (1980) and there is evidence that it also exists in south-eastern New South Wales. Although they are solitary animals they tend to be found reasonably close together in the dense forests. They sleep in a nest constructed of leaves and bark in a depression under vegetation. Illustrated on page 45.

Gilbert's Potoroo (*Potorous gilbertii*) [*gilbertii* refers to the naturalist Gilbert] Recently (1994), this potoroo was rediscovered at Two Peoples Bay Nature Reserve near Albany,

Western Australia. It is present in only a small area of habitat and has been given a critically endangered status. Its microhabitat preferences are currently being studied to ensure its future survival. It appears to utilise a variety of vegetation types, possibly requiring dense vegetation for shelter and protection from predators and preferring open areas for foraging. Illustrated on page 41.

Musky Rat-kangaroo (*Hypsiprymnodon moschatus*) [*hypsiprymnodon* = 'high-rumped', *moschatus* = 'musky odour'] This animal comes out in the early morning and at dusk and spends the rest of the day and night in a nest of dried leaves and ferns. It is found in the rainforests of Queensland, from just north of Townsville to around Trinity Bay, north of Cairns. Peculiarities of this species are that it has four, not two, incisors at the front of the bottom jaw (although two of these are vestigial) and still has five toes on the hind foot, with a thumb before the grooming toe on the inside of the foot like a possum—useful for climbing up and over the trunks and branches of fallen trees. Its diet consists of fruit, insects, worms, grasshoppers and so on that it finds in the leaf litter on the forest floor.

Another unusual feature of this species is that the female may have two young at a time. The female builds a maternity nest which is larger than a normal one; even after the young have become independent they may still use this nest while the mother moves on to another one. Musky Rat-kangaroos are unusual also in the way they move at speed with a quadrupedal action (using all four feet), where all other macropods use only their hindfeet when they are moving rapidly. They are generally solitary animals but occasionally two or three will be seen feeding near each other in the forest. The combined head and body length of the Musky Rat-kangaroo averages 23 cm and the average weight is about 520 g. Illustrated on page 33.

Bettongs

Australia originally boasted six species of bettongs but one, the **Desert Rat-kangaroo** (*Caloprymnus campestris*) [*caloprymnus* = 'beautiful rump', *campestris* = 'plain or field'] has been extinct since 1935 from the south-west of Queensland and the north-east of South Australia, where it lived in the hottest, driest and most exposed area of Australia, making flimsy nests on gibber plains and loamy flats with sparse saltbush vegetation. The remaining five species inhabit areas that include tussock and hummock grasses, clumped low understoreys with woody shrubs, and open dry sclerophyll forest with a grassy understorey. They are nocturnal, and prefer to feed in grassy areas. They rest and sleep in a depression under a bush or tussock, depending on the thick understorey for nesting. Bettongs and potoroos are the only macropods that possess a prehensile tail.

The bettongs' nests, made of grasses and bark which they carry in their prehensile tails, are oval, about 20 × 30 cm, with walls 2–3 cm thick and an entrance opening measuring about 5–10 cm. They are built in a 5 cm deep depression about 15 cm in diameter. Bettongs have from two to six nests each and rotate around them every few days, staying only 2 to 6 consecutive days in each.

Bettongs in general are solitary animals, though they will sometimes be seen feeding together on grasslands at night or be found in pairs in a nest (except in the case of the Tasmanian Bettong). The Burrowing Bettong digs a short, shallow curving tunnel that can have two entrances/exits, often forming huge warrens with many entrances. On Barrow Island off Western Australia one such complex with 120 exits is occupied by about 60 individuals. Their tunnels are usually built in loamy soils or in damper low-lying areas in deserts; often dug around outcrops of limestone or gypseous rock or under boulders or cap rock, and sometimes in cave floors. Brush-tailed Bettong females will share their nest with their young at foot until the next joey is permanently out of the pouch, when the older one is evicted.

The bettongs' main diet includes tubers, underground fungi, seeds, insects and bulbs. Some, like the Brush-tailed Bettong, also feed on the resin from hakea bushes while others, like the Tasmanian Bettong whose main diet consists of fungi, nibble exudates from acacia trees. Burrowing Bettongs will eat some green plants, fruit, nuts and termites, and on Barrow Island have been seen eating carrion. Bettongs drink little or no water as they get the moisture they require from their food sources.

European settlement, coupled with the introduction of foxes and rabbits, competition for land with pastoral developments and altered fire regimes, has led to the drastic decline of all the bettongs, except the Rufous, which seems to cope with some pastoral encroachments without being badly affected. Cats eliminated the Burrowing Bettong on Dirk Hartog Island and foxes played a major role in its elimination on the mainland in central and western Australia. The Western Shield Project, which carried out broadscale baiting with 1080 poison in Western Australia, has allowed the re-establishment of Brush-tailed Bettongs in many areas. Unfortunately the Desert Dreaming Project in the Gibson Desert in the early 1990s was not as successful. Burrowing Bettongs were introduced to the area, but probably due to

Rufous Bettong attempting to gather a length of wool in his tail to line his nest

the depredations of foxes and feral cats they all disappeared. The main native predators these smaller Potoroids have to contend with are the Masked Owl, Wedge-tailed Eagle, ospreys, goannas, pythons and quolls.

Rufous Bettong (*Aepyprymnus rufescens*) [*aepyprymnus* = 'high rumped', *rufescens* = 'reddish'] is still locally common in places along the east coast and mountains from the Cooktown area in southern Cape York to Lake Macquarie in New South Wales. It is uncommon and possibly extinct in the southern part of its range. Populations reported from the Victorian/New South Wales border south of Deniliquin are now considered extinct. Its range has otherwise not been as badly affected as those of the other bettongs and it seems to be holding its own reasonably well. It appears that the scrub tick keeps fox numbers low in areas where these bettongs occur. Illustrated on page 33.

Tasmanian Bettong (*Bettongia gaimardi*) [*bettongia* = 'small wallaby', *gaimardi* refers to the French naturalist Gaimard] Found only in Tasmania, being now totally extinct from the Australian mainland. This species omits insects from its diet although occasionally it might eat some accidentally while feeding on vegetation. The main part of its diet is fungal sporocarps, a specialised taste. For such a small animal this bettong has a large home range (from 65 to 136 hectares) enabling it to hunt for this very particular type of food, which is more abundant in burnt areas. Tasmanian Bettongs use different sets of nests in different seasons. Each set can include three to six nests which are usually only slept in for one or two nights at a time. Illustrated on page 46.

Brush-tailed Bettong (*Bettongia penicillata*) [*bettongia* = 'small wallaby', *penicillata* = 'brush-tailed'] This species used to inhabit much of southern Australia west of the Great Dividing Range, but is now very scarce, found only in three small areas in southern Western Australia around the Dryandra and Perup Forests and the Tuttanning Reserve. Illustrated on page 40.

Burrowing Bettong (*Bettongia lesueur*) [*bettongia* = 'small wallaby', *lesueur* refers to the French naturalist Le Sueur] This species was once found over most of Western Australia, South Australia, inland New South Wales and the Northern Territory, but is now restricted to Dorre and Bernier Islands in Shark Bay and Barrow Island in Western Australia. Inhabiting only 1 per cent of its former range, it is very rare and endangered. The main causes of its decline were the introduction of domestic stock, fire regime changes, competition for food by rabbits in drought times, predators such as the fox and cat, and disease. Illustrated on page 42.

Northern Brush-tailed Bettong (*Bettongia tropica*) [*bettongia* = 'small wallaby', *tropica* = 'tropical'] Found only in two isolated areas in northern Queensland, the Lamb Range east of Mareeba and west of Mossman on the Mount Windsor Tableland. Unconfirmed sightings have been reported around Mt Carbine, Ravenshoe and the Atherton area as well. These Bettongs are unusual in the fact that they only have two teats instead of the usual four. Illustrated on page 33.

Hare-wallabies

Of the five species of Hare-wallabies, two have become extinct in the last 100 years—the Brown (Eastern) and the Central species; and two are rare—the Rufous and the Banded. The only locally common species is the Spectacled Hare-wallaby.

Banded Hare-wallaby (*Lagostrophus fasciatus*) [*lagostrophus* = 'turning hare', *fasciatus* = 'banded'] Once inhabited south-western Western Australia but is now restricted to Bernier and Dorre Islands in Shark Bay. Its usual haunt is in dense *Acacia ligulata* bush where its runways lead to sheltered areas where the animals sleep during the daylight hours. They are socially compatible, but have distinct home ranges. They graze in open areas on grasses, malvaceous and leguminous shrubs and other plants. Illustrated on page 42.

Rufous Hare-wallaby (*Lagorchestes hirsutus*) [*lagorchestes* = 'dancing hare', *hirsutus* = 'hairy, shaggy'] Once common in arid and semi-arid areas in spinifex hummock grasslands of sand plains and sand-dune deserts, the Rufous Hare-wallaby's sole refuges now are on Dorre and Bernier Islands in Shark Bay, Western Australia, and a small area in the Tanami Desert in the south-western corner of the Northern Territory. They shelter by day in a trench dug under a spinifex hummock and in the hot summer months burrow to about 70 cm deep under these hummocks or sometimes under a teatree shrub.

The basic diet of this species is seeds, young sedge bulbs and leaves, grasses, fruit, insects, herbs and the young new leaves of various shrubs. New colonies are being established in the Tanami and regulated fires are being used to bring on the new young growth of vegetation that these animals favour. They are strictly nocturnal, solitary animals. Illustrated on page 42.

Spectacled Hare-wallaby (*Lagorchestes conspicillatus*) [*lagorchestes* = 'turning hare', *conspicillatus* = 'spectacled'] Populations of this hare-wallaby survive well in the tropical grasslands, open forest and woodlands, tall shrublands over tussock grass and grasslands of northern Australia. Even though less abundant, the Spectacled Hare-wallaby has not declined in numbers as greatly as the other hare-wallaby species. It appears to have declined in the Pilbara and Kimberley regions of Western Australia, is slowly disappearing from the hummock grass areas of central and eastern Northern Territory and is now extinct from the MacDonnell Ranges. Once again it is found in greatest abundance on Barrow Island; it is still classed as common in Queensland but rare in the Northern Territory.

Spectacled Hare-wallabies browse on shrubs and the tips of spinifex leaves when they venture out of their hideaways in the spinifex hummocks at night. Like most hare-wallabies they drink little or no water. Illustrated on page 33.

Nailtail wallabies

Of the three species of nailtail wallabies, the Crescent Nailtail is extinct, the Bridled Nailtail is rare, and only the Northern Nailtail is locally common. These wallabies get their distinctive name from the fingernail-like growth on the tip of their tail. They also possess very long claws, used for digging resting hollows under vegetation, which also assist them in climbing into hollow trees or logs when they are pursued by a predator, an escape route known to have been used by the Crescent Nailtail and still used by the Bridled Nailtail Wallaby.

Bridled Nailtail Wallaby (*Onychogalea fraenata*) [*onychogalea* = 'nailed weasel', *fraenata* = 'bridle'] This animal's range used to extend from inland of Charters Towers in Queensland to the Murray River, but it is now restricted to a reserve near Dingo in Queensland. They inhabit open eucalypt forest, woodland and brigalow bush, where they graze on ferns, herbs and grasses at dusk and during the night. During the day they rest in scrapes or depressions dug under a bush or tree. This species is one of Australia's rarest macropods and was thought to be extinct until 1973 when this remaining colony was rediscovered. The last previous sighting was in 1931. It is now conserved in an 11 000 hectare refuge, land that was bought specifically for this species' survival. This wallaby is a solitary animal which hides in dense brigalow scrub during the day where it can escape from predators. Its decline is attributed mainly to competition for food by stock, the destruction of groundcover and the effects of predation by feral cats (still active against the Dingo population). Illustrated on page 37.

Northern Nailtail Wallaby (*Onychogalea unguifera*) [*onychogalea* = 'nailed weasel', *unguifera* = 'nail bearing'] This wallaby lives in lightly wooded flood plains in the northern part of Western Australia, the Northern Territory and Queensland, but avoids the highest rainfall areas. In the southern areas of its range it favours open long-grass woodlands and savannah and appears to be common in paperbark scrub on the edges of the open plains near Broome, Western Australia. In general this animal is solitary but groups can be seen feeding together between dusk and dawn. This species has not been as greatly affected by European settlement as the other two species. Illustrated on page 37.

Rock-wallabies

Rock-wallabies are found on the Australian mainland and offshore islands but not in Tasmania, even though suitable habitats are available. These wallabies are often distinctly coloured and patterned and live in very rocky habitats with deep cracks, caves and tumbled boulders. Males and females have the same markings, but females are usually only about two-thirds the size of males. The females breed continually once they reach sexual maturity between one and two years of age. Rock-wallabies range in size from the Nabarlek, 29 cm from nose to base of tail, to the Yellow-footed and the Proserpine, both 65 cm from nose to base of tail.

Some species of rock-wallaby in the extremely arid areas are adapted to drinking no water at all, partly due to the fact that they shelter in caves where the humidity is higher and the temperature is 10–15°C (20–30°F) cooler than outside. They usually emerge in the late afternoon and feed all night, followed by a short bask in the early morning sun, especially after cool nights. They feed on grassy areas either on top of or at the base of cliffs, or on flat terraces among the rocks where they will also eat herbs, leaves and fruits.

The claw on the outside toe of these very agile wallabies is very short and they have a very granulated, softish pad under the foot for added grip on the slippery, rocky terrain that they rapidly and so precariously move about on. They use their forepaws when making extra long leaps to get a safer foothold on a ledge or ridge that may sometimes be no more than 15 cm wide, and hop up very steep sloping rock faces and sloping tree trunks. The tail is quite long and less tapering than the tail of other wallabies; it is carried arched over the back for balance when the animal is hopping.

A habit unique to rock-wallabies concerns their young at foot when they are permanently out of the pouch: these young are left in a shelter in their rocky environment to which the mother returns regularly for the young to suckle, rather than the young following the mother about as in most other macropod species.

Rock-wallaby numbers have declined since European settlement in many areas; in conjunction with the introduction of rabbits and goats which has caused competition for food and shelter, predation by foxes and occasionally cats, added to predation by man for their pelts, has caused major problems. The main native predator of rock-wallabies is the Wedge-tailed Eagle, which can sometimes be seen dive-bombing a wallaby in an attempt to kill it or make it fall and thus end up as the eagle's next meal.

Some species, like the Black-footed Rock-wallaby, have developed from another specific species after becoming isolated from the parent population by topographic change. In this way small groups have evolved within their own rocky outcrops to become sub-species or different races. With the introduction of stock paddocks and crops, intervening corridors of vegetation have been destroyed and such groups have become further isolated.

Allied Rock-wallaby (*Petrogale assimilis*) [*petrogale* = 'rock-weasel', *assimilis* = 'similar'] Widespread in north-eastern Queensland from Home Hill to Croydon, and south-west to Hughenden. There are also colonies on Magnetic and Palm Islands. Within this species, adult males and females will form pairs, share their feeding and sleeping areas and engage in mutual grooming sessions. Illustrated on page 17.

Black-footed Rock-wallaby (*Petrogale lateralis lateralis*) [*petrogale* = 'rock-weasel', *lateralis lateralis* = 'notable-sided'] Within this species there are now four sub-species and two races. The Black-footed Rock-wallaby was originally described in 1842 in Western Australia. It used to be widespread throughout the southern half of Western Australia but is now found only in five isolated areas—on Barrow Island, on Salisbury Island in the Recherche Archipelago, in the Calvert Ranges in the Little Sandy Desert in central Western Australia, on North-West Cape and in colonies scattered in the wheatbelt in south-west Western Australia. Illustrated on page 17. **Hackett's Rock-wallaby** (*Petrogale lateralis hacketti*) was formally described in 1905 in the Recherche Archipelago islands off the coast of southern Western Australia and the larger **Purple-collared Rock-wallaby** (*Petrogale lateralis purpurecollis*) from western Queensland was first described in 1924. This group gets its name from a purple coloured secretion varying in intensity on the head, neck and shoulders. Illustrated on page 17 and 36. In 1922 a small group in South Australia, the **Pearson Island Rock-wallaby** (*Petrogale lateralis pearsonii*), was described as a separate species. There are two other isolated races, one in the Kimberley region and one in the MacDonnell Ranges, but they both fit into the main *lateralis* group. Illustrated on page 44.

Brush-tailed Rock-wallaby (*Petrogale penicillata penicillata*) [*petrogale* = 'rock weasel', *penicillata penicillata* = 'brush-tailed'] This is eastern Australia's most abundant species, although in Victoria it is becoming rare and possibly endangered. The Brush-tailed Rock-wallaby inhabits the ranges just north of the Queensland/New South Wales border and follows the Great Dividing Range down into northern Victoria. Most of the rocky outcrops favoured by this rock-wallaby face north, as they enjoy basking in the early morning and evening sun. Brush-tailed Rock-wallabies were so abundant in the early 1900s that over 92 000 skins were sold through one Sydney business alone in 1908; between 1884 and 1914 bounties were paid for over half a million rock-wallaby pelts.

Australia is not the only country where this rock-wallaby is found; in 1916 a pair escaped from a collection on the Hawaiian Island of Oahu and established a successful population in the valleys and on the rocky slopes, which by 1981 numbered about 250. Since then numbers have declined to between 80–100, possibly because of inbreeding. Brush-tailed Rock-wallabies were also released onto Kawau, Rangitoto and Motutapu Islands off New Zealand, where they have become a pest and have to be regularly culled. Illustrated on page 20.

Cape York Rock-wallaby (*Petrogale coenensis*) [*petrogale* = 'rock weasel', *coenensis* = from the name Coen] A rare species that is found only on the north-eastern part of Cape York between Musgrave and the Pascoe River. Very few animals of this species have been seen and it appears to be rare and very scattered within its range.

Godman's Rock-wallaby (*Petrogale godmani*) [*petrogale* = 'rock weasel', *godmani* from the name Godman] Found in the eastern half of southern Cape York from Bathurst Head south to the Mitchell River and across to Mt Carbine near the coast. It appears to be closely related to *P. assimilis* and *P. coenensis* and there are also some similarities with *P. mareeba*.

Herbert's Rock-wallaby (*Petrogale herberti*) [*petrogale* = 'rock weasel', *herberti* from the name Herbert] This common species ranges over a wide area of south-eastern Queensland from just north of Rubyvale and Clermont across to the Fitzroy River's southern bank in Rockhampton and then southwards to Nanango. Herbert's Rock-wallaby is equivalent in appearance to a cross between *P. penicillata* from the south and *P. inornata* from the north. Illustrated on page 20.

Allied Rock-wallaby (*Petrogale assimilis*) (Dennis Browning)

Black-footed Rock-wallaby (*Petrogale lateralis lateralis*), Western Australia (Arthur White)

Black-footed Rock-wallaby (*Petrogale lateralis purpurecollis*), Queensland (Rob Close)

Mareeba Rock-wallaby (*Petrogale mareeba*) [*petrogale* = 'rock weasel', *mareeba* from the name of the town] Found in a fairly small area of Queensland, from the Mitchell River near Mt Carbine, west to Mungana, with its southern boundary being the Burdekin River near Mt Garnet. The fur colour of these animals varies in different populations. Animals that live on basalt rocks are almost black while those that live on lighter-coloured rocks have evolved a light coloured coat that matches the rocky outcrops of their surroundings.

Monjon Rock-wallaby (*Petrogale burbidgei*) [*petrogale* = 'rock weasel', *burbidgei* from the name Burbidge] This, almost the smallest of the rock-wallabies, measuring only 30–35 cm from nose to base of tail, was only recently discovered (1970s). Its habitat is restricted to inhospitable areas of the Kimberley region in Western Australia where it can easily be confused with the Nabarlek/Little Rock-wallaby. It is common but limited in King Leopold sandstone country along the coastline and on Bigge, Katers and Boongaree Islands in the Bonaparte Archipelago off the north coast of Western Australia. Illustrated on page 21.

Nabarlek/Little Rock-wallaby (*Peradorcas concinna*) [*peradorcas* = 'marsupial gazelle', *concinna* = 'elegant'] The smallest of the rock-wallabies, this species is broken into three sub-species: one in east Arnhem Land, another in the north-east corner of Western Australia and the third in the north-west Victoria Rivers area on the Western Australia/Northern Territory border. During the wet season these animals actually become quite diurnal, staying out for three hours after dawn and feeding for several hours before dusk. In the dry season the Nabarlek will venture quite a distance, several hundred metres, from its rocky shelter to feed on the fern nardoo (*Marsilea crenata*) that grows on the black soil plains. The White-bellied Sea-eagle regularly preys on these small wallabies. Illustrated on page 20.

Proserpine Rock-wallaby (*Petrogale persephone*) [*petrogale* = 'rock weasel', *persephone* = Proserpine] This species appears to be more closely related to the Yellow-footed Rock-wallaby than any other species. Its status is vulnerable/endangered as it has only a very small range and was only really described in 1976. The Proserpine Rock-wallaby could once have been more widespread, as it appears that the more adaptable Unadorned Rock-wallaby may have partly contributed to its decline, much as has happened in the case of the decline of Godman's Rock-wallaby of Cape York. The males of the Proserpine species are about 50 per cent larger than the females. Very little is known about its breeding habits but it does appear to have a continuous breeding season.

Rothschild's Rock-wallaby (*Petrogale rothschildi*) [*petrogale* = 'rock weasel', *rothschildi* after Lord Rothschild] Lord Rothschild supported the expedition that found the first specimen in 1901. This is one of the larger species and is reasonably common where it lives in Western Australia around the Hamersley Range. Its distribution appears to be limited to granite rock piles and outcrops where the temperature can be up to 15°C lower than the outside heat in some of the deep caves. It used to live on Lewis Island in the Dampier Archipelago but has now become extinct. There are colonies on Dolphin, Rosemary and Enderby Islands, and West Lewis Island has been restocked from the Enderby population. Illustrated on page 20.

Sharman's Rock-wallaby (*Petrogale sharmani*) [*petrogale* = 'rock weasel', *sharmani* after the researcher G. B. Sharman] This rock-wallaby lives in an area totalling 200 000 hectares in the Seaview and Coane Ranges west of Ingham, Queensland. It is almost impossible to distinguish this species from *P. assimilis* and *P. mareeba* except by genetic analysis.

Short-eared Rock-wallaby (*Petrogale brachyotis*) [*petrogale* = 'rock weasel', *brachyotis* = 'short-eared'] Found across the northern parts of Western Australia and the Northern Territory, from the Kimberley area through Arnhem Land to partway around the Gulf of Carpentaria. This species lives on low rocky hills, cliffs and gorges associated with savannah grassland and is extremely variable in colour pattern and size. Because of this variability the Short-eared Rock-wallaby has been separated into three races—the Kimberley, the Victoria River and the Arnhem Land races. Although they are reasonably common they live in isolated groups that are vulnerable if the habitat is didturbed. They are extinct on the western edge of their former range. Illustrated on page 21.

Unadorned Rock-wallaby (*Petrogale inornata*) [*petrogale* = 'rock weasel', *inornata* = 'unadorned'] This species occurs in open sclerophyll forests with associated rocky areas along the Great Dividing Range in Queensland, from Home Hill near Ayr south to the northern bank of the Fitzroy River at Rockhampton, and also inhabits some of the Whitsunday Islands. Illustrated on page 21.

Yellow-footed Rock-wallaby (*Petrogale xanthopus*) [*petrogale* = 'rock weasel', *xanthopus* = 'yellow-footed'] One of the largest species, the Yellow-footed Rock-wallaby is common in suitable habitat in the Gawler and Flinders Ranges of South Australia, and limited and rare in the Barrier Ranges in South Australia and western New South Wales. The sub-species *P. x. celeris* in the Grey Range in south-west Queensland is also reasonably common where suitable habitat exists. This species is one of the inland varieties that live in dry arid areas associated with Mulga scrub and because of its very colourful coat pattern has been hunted for its skin. In 1896 Lydekker reported that '100's of skins were imported to London from Adelaide annually along with Brush-tailed Rock-wallaby skins'. Illustrated on page 20.

Quokka

Quokka (*Setonix brachyurus*) [*setonix* = 'bristle-footed', *brachyurus* = 'short-tailed'] Quokkas are found in the south-west of Western Australia, including Rottnest and Bald Islands. Even though Quokkas prefer dense moist vegetation, they survive reasonably well on Rottnest Island which is very harsh and seasonally arid with low vegetation and a scarcity of fresh water. The plants they feed on become very low on nitrogen and water through the summer months, with the result that many animals become anaemic and die by the end of summer, particularly those farthest from fresh water, but because of successful breeding rates they still maintain a stable population. This species forms group territories consisting of 25 to 150 adults and very few individuals move away from a territory. Quokkas fight each other for shelter around water sources in very hot weather and males will defend their sleeping sites against intruders. Illustrated on page 42.

Pademelons

Pademelons are very compact little wallabies with short limbs. They usually live in dense undergrowth in rainforests and wet sclerophyll forests, using tunnel-like runways to move about, grazing on grasses and browsing on shrubs. Where the habitat has been badly disturbed, their numbers have declined; however, selective logging practices in general do not bother them. In fact, where suitable habitat exists they can at times become over-populated; e.g. in Tasmania they are culled because of apparent damage to pastoral lands.

There are three species in this family—the Red-legged Pademelon, found along the coastal and eastern ranges of Queensland, from Cape York down to northern New South Wales; the Red-necked Pademelon, found from Gympie in southern Queensland to the Watagan Mountains near Gosford in New South Wales; and the Tasmanian Pademelon, now found only in Tasmania since becoming extinct in Victoria.

Red-legged Pademelon (*Thylogale stigmatica*) [*thylogale* = 'pouched weasel', *stigmatica* = 'pricked pattern'] This is the most colourful of the three pademelons, with rufous brown colouring on its cheeks, arms and hindlegs. It is usually solitary, but groups of up to four animals can be seen feeding together on fruits that have fallen to the forest floor. They browse quite a bit on fishbone fern and king orchids, while the Moreton Bay Fig also appears to be important in their diet. There are three sub-species of the Red-legged Pademelon in Australia plus one in the southern central highlands of New Guinea. Illustrated on pages 34 and 39.

Red-necked Pademelon (*Thylogale thetis*) [*thylogale* = 'pouched weasel', *thetis* refers to a French vessel sailing in Australian waters in 1825] This animal has reddish colouration only around its neck and on its shoulders and is very similar to the Red-legged in living habits. Some will travel up to 2 km from their sleeping areas, where they lie in shallow depressions on the forest floor, to feeding sites where there can be up to ten grazing at a time. As do all pademelons, when disturbed they scatter individually back into the forest. Because of their short limbs, pademelons do not need to use the tail for support when walking slowly on all fours—it just drags behind them. Illustrated on pages 34 and 39.

Tasmanian Pademelon (*Thylogale billardierii*) [*thylogale* = 'pouched weasel', *billardierii* refers to the botanist La Billardière] This pademelon is widely spread over Tasmania and the larger Bass Strait Islands. It inhabits dry sclerophyll forests as long as there are moist gullies or patches of sedge, etc. to provide shelter during the day. They are also found in snowfall areas where they sometimes have to dig away the snow to get food, usually under trees where the snow is not as deep. Illustrated on page 46.

Wallabies

Swamp Wallaby (*Wallabia bicolor*) [*wallabia* = 'small kangaroo', *bicolor* = 'two-coloured'] This macropod is very different from the *Macropus* genus—genetically, reproductively, dentally and behaviourally. All other species in this group have 16 chromosomes, but male Swamp Wallabies have 11 chromosomes and females 10, which places them in the separate genus *Wallabia*.

Swamp Wallabies live in thick understorey vegetation in forests, woodlands and heath in eastern Australia from the tip of Cape York down the coast and ranges through New South Wales and into the forests in over half of Victoria. They prefer to browse on shrubs and coarse vegetation which may explain why they, as well as the Agile Wallaby, have a broad premolar that is never shed (see page 12 for diagram). The Swamp Wallaby is the only marsupial with a gestation period (33–38 days) longer than its oestrous cycle.

Wallabies are small to medium-sized kangaroos. When these wallabies rest or sleep they usually sit hunched with their hind legs and tail out in front of them; occasionally they sleep on their sides like the larger kangaroo species. Illustrated on page 39.

Agile Wallaby (*Macropus agilis*) [*macropus* = 'long foot', *agilis* = 'agile'] This wallaby is the most widespread macropod in tropical Australia where it inhabits grasslands and forests along rivers and creeks; in the Northern Territory it is prolific from the coast to the rugged inland hills. The Agile Wallaby is gregarious, living in groups of up to ten animals, but congregates into even larger groups while feeding on grasses and sedges and digging for roots of certain grasses. It is quite a nervous animal and does a lot of foot-thumping when alarmed. The Agile Wallaby has been labelled as a pest animal because of its abundance and the damage it causes to crops and pasturelands. Illustrated on page 34.

Brush-tailed Rock-wallaby (*Petrogale penicillata penicillata*)

Yellow-footed Rock-wallaby (*Petrogale xanthopus*) (Tanya Williams)

Herbert's Rock-wallaby (*Petrogale herberti*) (Rob Close)

Nabarlek / Little Rock-wallaby (*Peradorcas concinna*) (G.D. Sanson/Nature Focus)

Rothschild's Rock-wallaby (*Petrogale rothschildi*) (Gerry Maynes)

Monjon Rock-wallaby (*Petrogale burbidgei*) (Malcolm Douglas/Nature Focus)

Short-eared Rock-wallaby (*Petrogale brachyotis*) (Sandy Ingleby)

Unadorned Rock-wallaby (*Petrogale inornata*). The Sharman's, Mareeba and Godman's Rock-wallabies are very similar in appearance to the Unadorned Rock-wallaby (Ian Morris)

Black-striped Wallaby (*Macropus dorsalis*) [*macropus* = 'long foot', *dorsalis* = 'notably-backed'] Abundant in south-east Queensland, to Rockhampton in the north and west to Charleville, and south to the Clarence River catchment area near Acacia Plateau and Urbenville. They are very gregarious and form groups of twenty individuals or more. When they are disturbed they run off as a group in one direction and unless they are persistently pursued, will not separate. They use very well formed pathways through vegetation and across grasslands and appear to be very adaptable, as much of their original habitat has been changed or destroyed. The Black-striped Wallaby remains abundant in Queensland and in some areas it is classed as a pest species, but in New South Wales it is now listed as endangered in the Threatened Species Conservation Act, 1995. Illustrated on page 37.

Parma Wallaby (*Macropus parma*) [*macropus* = 'long foot', *parma* = Aboriginal name] This wallaby was believed to be extinct on mainland Australia during the 1900s and a large colony on Kawau Island off New Zealand was thought to hold the only living specimens. However, in the late 1960s a female was found near Gosford and following surveys of the forests of New South Wales it was found to occur in wet and dry forests from the Gibraltar Range in northern New South Wales south to the Watagan Mountains near Gosford; in the past, it was found as far south as Bega near the Victorian border. Although generally a solitary animal, where large populations do occur the animals congregate to feed on suitable grassy areas within moist forests (e.g. Dingo State Forest near Wingham), but they disperse individually when disturbed. Illustrated on page 39.

Red-necked Wallaby (*Macropus rufogriseus*) [*macropus* = 'long foot', *rufogriseus* = 'red-grey'] This is a common wallaby found in eucalypt forests in south-eastern Australia, Tasmania and its adjacent islands. This species forms small groups of about six to ten animals and can often be seen grazing on the forest edges in the late afternoon. Earlier this century, the Red-necked Wallaby was commonly sent overseas to zoos and parks as it breeds very easily in captivity. Many years ago it was released, and subsequently formed colonies, in Germany, but during World War I this population was shot and used for food. In Derbyshire, England, a pair escaped from a private zoo in the 1940s and became well established, until the severely cold winter of 1962–63 reduced the population to about six individuals. They were also released near Waimate in New Zealand, where efforts are now being made to eradicate them because they have become a pest.

The first month or two after the young are permanently out of the pouch they do not venture out into the open grassy areas with their mother, but tend to stay under or near vegetation on the edges. This behaviour is common to many of the wallaby species. Illustrated on page 37.

Tammar Wallaby (*Macropus eugenii*) [*macropus* = 'long foot', *eugenii* refers to the name of the island Eugene (now St Peter) on which it was first found] These wallabies are found on more than ten offshore islands where they are common, but on the mainland in Western Australia and South Australia they are rare. The animals found on Flinders Island, South Australia, were slimmer and more delicate, with a shorter sleeker coat, but this population is now extinct, due to bushfires, loss of habitat and predation by feral cats. The members of the population on Kangaroo Island, South Australia, are physically larger than any of the other Tammar populations in Australia. They feed on grassy areas associated with low dense vegetation where they shelter during the day, emerging after dark and returning before dawn. It has been found that Tammar Wallabies can survive by drinking seawater when fresh water is not available.

The Tammar Wallaby is only one of three species of macropods that show a distinct seasonal breeding pattern. Young are usually born in late January after which the female is mated. An embryo is held internally until the following January; if for some reason the pouch joey dies before June the embryo is stimulated to develop and is born. No young are ever born in the months from July to December, even though the pouch young are permanently out of the pouch in October. Females become sexually mature at about nine months while they are still suckling from their mother, but any mating will still not produce a young until January of the following year. Illustrated on page 40.

Western Brush/Black-gloved Wallaby (*Macropus irma*) [*macropus* = 'long foot', *irma* meaning unknown) Known only from south-western Western Australia, this wallaby prefers a more open habitat than most wallabies where it grazes instead of browsing. Inhabiting open woodlands and forest with low grasses and open thickets, it sometimes utilises mallee areas and heathland as well. It is an early morning/late afternoon grazer and rests during the hottest parts of the day in the shade of vegetation, either alone or in pairs. This wallaby does not appear to need water. When necessary it moves very rapidly, with the ability to weave and dodge obstacles easily as it keeps low to the ground.

During the 1970s foxes increased dramatically in numbers and the Brush Wallaby population dropped by about 80 per cent, so it is now classed as uncommon in its range. There was a marked increase in populations when foxes were controlled. Illustrated on page 40.

Whiptail/Pretty-faced Wallaby (*Macropus parryi*) [*macropus* = 'long foot', *parryi* after Captain Parry] This wallaby's range, in open forests with a grassy understorey, extends from just south of Cooktown to denser populations in its southern habitats around the Queensland/New South Wales border to as far south as Kempsey, New South Wales, where it is now rare. This species tends to spend most of the day feeding, especially in the early morning and evening, on grasses, herbs and some ferns. It appears to get most of its moisture from dew and vegetation, as it very rarely drinks.

Whiptails are often found in groups of 10–50 animals which are broken down into many sub-groups of mixed animals, adults, sub-adults and young of both sexes. When alarmed the wallabies run as a group in a zig-zag fashion. When a female is in oestrous there is usually a line of males following her with the dominant one closest to her. He often puts on a dominance display by pulling up clods of grass with his forepaws while staring down his opposition.

The clearing of land by farmers for agriculture or pasture has probably helped to provide more feeding areas for this species as cleared land suits their habits as long as some tree cover is still available. Illustrated on page 38.

Large kangaroos

All the large macropods are quite abundant within their ranges. In fact, European settlement has meant that more water has been provided, by dams and bores, especially for the kangaroos living in arid areas. More food sources with the development of agricultural land has increased their populations over the last two hundred years.

Red Kangaroos and Eastern and Western Grey Kangaroos are the three species usually shot and harvested for food, pelts and as pests in agricultural areas.

Antilopine Wallaroo (*Macropus antilopinus*) [*macropus* = 'long foot', *antilopinus* = 'antelope haired'] In appearance this wallaroo is a cross between the Euro and the Red or Grey Kangaroo. It has longer legs and is less stocky than either the Common or Black Wallaroos. The Antilopine Wallaroo inhabits the woodlands in tropical areas in the north of Australia where Red and Grey Kangaroos are absent. It is a common species, especially in Arnhem Land, where it feeds on grasses on relatively flat land, but can be seen at waterholes in hilly areas where the Black and the Common Wallaroo are also found. They are quite gregarious and will be seen in groups of up to 30 individuals, although usually the groups are smaller than this, about 10 members.

The Antilopine Wallaroo will feed at any time of the day or night, depending on the temperature. It does not like to be out in the open on very hot days, when it will rest among trees or shrubbery or in rocky areas, usually near a water supply. These animals live in quite dense populations, varying from 11.4 to 30.9 animals per square kilometre in the wet season down to 8.9 to19.0 animals per square kilometre in the dry season. Illustrated on pages 35 and 43.

Black Wallaroo (*Macropus bernardus*) [*macropus* = 'long foot', *bernardus* from the name Bernard] Described only in recent years in Kakadu National Park, the Black Wallaroo, the smallest of the euro/wallaroo family, has one of the smallest distributions of any kangaroo in Australia, living only in the rugged north-western part of the Arnhem Plateau, where it is quite common. If the animals are disturbed during the day they are gone before you even see them, hopping off among the rocky outcrops of the escarpment. Very little is known about this species except that they are strictly nocturnal and feed in small groups in grassy valleys at night, preferring to sleep alone during the day in their cool rocky habitat where they can see danger approaching. Illustrated on page 43.

Common Wallaroo/Euro (*Macropus robustus*) [*macropus* = 'long foot', *robustus* = 'robust'] These animals live a solitary life, favouring areas that include caves, rocky outcrops, ledges in escarpments and rocky hillsides, although they tend to congregate around waterholes. They have a very long-haired shaggy appearance and need to shelter from the heat in these rocky habitats, especially in central and western Australia. Their diet consists of grasses and shrubbery which they feed on during the cooler evenings on the slopes and plains near their rocky shelters. They do need to drink fresh water if they cannot get enough moisture from vegetation and avoid the heat sufficiently.

The Common Wallaroo inhabits most of Australia with the exception of western Cape York, southern Western Australia, some southern areas of South Australia, and all of Victoria and Tasmania.

The populations that live on the eastern and western slopes of the Great Dividing Range are distinctively coloured. The males are usually a very dark grey or black with the females being a much softer grey colour, although around Collinsville in northern Queensland, where the Ranges flatten and are near the coast, we have seen a mixture of coat colours, from the grey and black of the Common Wallaroo through to the reddish colours of the Euro. The populations west of the Great Dividing Range, right across to the Western Australian coast, have a shorter, more reddish coat, which blends in better with the colour of the habitat. Population densities for these kangaroos can range as high as 13 animals per square kilometre, but can be as low as 0.04. Males tend to range over areas three times as large as the females in summer, centred around rocky outcrops and/or a water source. Illustrated on page 43.

Eastern Grey Kangaroo (*Macropus giganteus*) [*macropus* = 'long foot', *giganteus* = 'gigantic'] The first specimens of these animals were taken in 1770 when the early explorers visited Australian shores near Cooktown, Queensland. They range over a variety of habitats, from coastal forests to the more arid inland where the annual rainfall is 250 mm+. Its distribution starts halfway up Cape York and extends down to cover two-thirds of Queensland, almost all of New South

Wales and Victoria and the north-east corner of Tasmania.

The Eastern Grey Kangaroo is gregarious in habit, often congregating into groups of 20 or more. Their food preferences are limited to grasses and forbs which are eaten usually from late afternoon to early morning in open paddocks or grasslands, with the rest of the day spent lying in the shade of trees and shrubs.

Female Grey Kangaroos, unlike most of the other macropods, do not put their tail out in front of them when they give birth—instead they lean back on it and push their hindfeet forward and upwards so that they are resting on their heels. The mortality rate for joeys in their first year can be very high. In one group that was studied for more than a year only three out of 30 joeys survived.

The only population of Grey Kangaroos in possible danger of extinction is the Tasmanian species (*M. g. tasmaniensis*) because it inhabits pastoral areas in north-eastern Tasmania where there is pressure from owners to cull them regularly—at the moment the population stands at about 20 000. Illustrated on page 35.

Western Grey Kangaroo (*Macropus fuliginosus*) [*macropus* = 'long foot', *fuliginosus* = 'sooty'] This species ranges from north of the Murchison River in Western Australia down to the southern coastline, across South Australia (including Kangaroo Island), and over the western half of Victoria and New South Wales, with populations creeping into central southern Queensland.

The Western Grey Kangaroo's coat is browner than that of the Eastern Grey Kangaroo, and it has a dark muzzle, hence it is often called the Black-faced Grey Kangaroo. They are sometimes called 'stinkers' as the males have quite a strong body odour. They graze mainly on quite coarse grasses and browse on a select species of shrubs. These kangaroos are gregarious, forming groups of 3 to 16 members. They can sometimes be seen in mixed groups with Eastern Grey Kangaroos in western and central New South Wales.

The Western Grey Kangaroo's breeding strategy differs from that of the Eastern Grey in that it does not have a delayed implantation function. This means that temporary stopping of the development of the embryo does not occur, thus the female does not mate until after the previous young has left the pouch permanently. This species is a seasonal breeder with most of the births occurring in summer and autumn. Illustrated on page 35.

Red Kangaroo (*Macropus rufus*) [*macropus* = 'long foot', *rufus* = 'red'] The Red Kangaroo is renowned as the desert kangaroo even though it prefers to eat green vegetation. Its range extends from the coast of Western Australia down to the Great Australian Bight, up to the Gulf in the Normanton area of Queensland to just over the north-western border of Victoria and east to the central-western slopes of New South

Wales and Queensland. We have also seen them 70 km from the east coast at Collinsville, south-west of Bowen in Queensland.

Red Kangaroos move about their habitat, foraging for green herbage in groups of 10 or more that usually include a dominant male. These animals are very dependent on a constant food and water supply for breeding and the survival of their young. If vegetation becomes scarce, the breeding cycle slows down, eventually ceasing if drought conditions persist. Fifty per cent of females stop breeding after just three months without rain in summer, five months in winter. Pouch young survival is even more drastically affected, with half of the pouch young dying after only a couple of months of drought. Illustrated on page 35.

Tree-kangaroos

The tree-kangaroos have a totally different body shape to other macropods, the result of their adaptation to living in the rainforests of tropical Queensland and New Guinea. There are two species in Australia and six or more species in New Guinea. The tree-kangaroos most commonly seen in zoos are two of the New Guinea species, the Matchie's and Goodfellow's tree-kangaroos which have reddish-brown and yellowish colouring, whereas the Australian mainland species is grey/brown/black in colour. The tree-kangaroo's cylindrical, non-tapering tail is very long in proportion to its body, and is used as a balance when moving about the tree tops. Their forearms are much larger and longer than those of other macropods, being more comparable to the koala's forelimbs, with long heavy claws and a very strong build. Their hindlimbs are shorter and sturdier, with much shorter, broader feet and toes than the hopping macropods.

Tree-kangaroos are very efficient climbers, using their long claws to grip onto the trunks and branches while going forwards or backwards with the hind legs, which move independently of each other. These are the only macropods which have this ability in normal daily movements. (Only when kangaroos swim do they move each hind leg alternately. Some kangaroos will shuffle their feet individually forwards or backwards but not over a long distance.) Tree-kangaroos hop, holding their forelimbs against their body, along very horizontal broad branches or on the ground. They sometimes use a quadrupedal movement on the ground, but this is usually in slower, walking mode. They descend from a tree by coming down the trunk backwards, hand over hand, with their hind feet sliding down the tree until they are about two metres from the ground, when they jump and twist around ready to move off as soon as they hit the ground. Some have been known to jump from a 15 metre height when disturbed.

In general tree-kangaroos are leaf-eaters, particularly favouring ribbonwood trees and wild tobacco (introduced), with the addition of various fruits and sometimes even maize from the local farms. Their hands are adapted to grabbing branches from which they eat the leaves and fruit while they hold the branch between their forepaws.

Male tree-kangaroos are very territorial. Most of them show scars from battles fought while defending their territories (up to 25 hectares) that overlap with several female territories. The young usually stay with their mothers for up to two years, so females and young are often seen in groups of three, whereas adult males are solitary and only visit their harems at night while they forage for food.

The fur on the tree-kangaroo's back is arranged so that when the animal is sleeping or resting during tropical rainstorms the rain runs straight off, leaving the underfur quite dry. Daytime is usually spent curled up on a branch in a sunny position quite high in the tree canopy away from their regular predators, the dingo and the Amethystine Python. The python, of course, is an efficient climber of trees and does catch up with many independent juveniles.

Bennett's Tree-kangaroo (*Dendrolagus bennettianus*) [*dendrolagus* = 'tree-hare', *bennettianus* from the name Bennett] The Bennett's Tree-kangaroo is sparsely distributed within its territory, from its southern boundary at the Daintree River to 75 km north to Mount Amos, and west 50 km from the coastal rainforests to the Mount Windsor Tablelands. In the northern part of their range they are quite common, but not in the southern section, where roads and developments have destroyed and broken up their habitat. In lowland rainforests this species feeds on the leaves of *Ganophyllum*, *Aidia*, *Schefflera*, Pisonia vine and Platycerium ferns and the fruit of *Chionanthus*, *Olea* and several types of figs. Illustrated on page 34.

Lumholtz's Tree-kangaroo (*Dendrolagus lumholtzi*) [*dendrolagus* = 'tree-hare', *lumholtzi* from the name Lumholtz] This species is no longer very common in the coastal lowland rainforest, being more populous in the higher altitude rainforests on the Atherton Tableland, between Kirrama and Mount Spurgeon. Its habitat has been restricted and is being further reduced by highland logging practices, but in the national parks and reserves it is holding its own quite well. Illustrated on this page and page 34.

A Lumholtz's Tree-kangaroo balancing precariously on a branch using its tail as a counterbalance, and showing the distinctive black facial mask and feet (Ian Morris)

· 3 ·
Reproduction

Breeding seasons

Most of the macropod species are continuous breeders. The exceptions include the Musky Rat-kangaroo, Bennett's and Lumholtz's Tree-kangaroos, the Quokka, the Tammar Wallaby, Western Brush Wallaby and the Black Wallaroo. The Red-necked Wallaby is a continuous breeder on the mainland, but is seasonal in Tasmania (possibly because of the colder winter). The Tammar Wallaby notably has a definite breeding season in January when all the young are born. If the January young is lost before the end of June, another will be born; a loss any later means that another young will not be born until the following January. The Bennett's (Red-necked) Wallaby in Tasmania gives birth only from late January to early August—in other words, if a female is mated during August the blastocyst will remain dormant until late December, appearing as a foetus near the end of January.

Competition for hierarchy

The breeding season is a time when males will fight each other for their position in the hierarchy and the privilege of mating the females approaching oestrous. The large kangaroos stand up on their hind legs and tail, and wrestle and kick at each other. The skin on their stomachs is particularly tough and can withstand quite a barrage of kicks with serious injury rarely occurring, as one of the combatants usually gives in, uttering a loud cough, before moving out of the victorious male's territory. The injuries that do occur are loss of fur and occasional cuts caused by the long claws on their forepaws. Smaller wallabies fight differently, often ending up grappling with each other and scrabbling with their hind feet. Sometimes they roll around on the ground locked together.

Inbreeding within a group does not usually occur because sub-adult males disperse into male-only groups or wander off to join another group where, when they are old enough, they may vie for mating privileges.

Mating procedure

A male usually approaches a female from the rear, sniffing her urogenital opening and her urine to test if she is coming into oestrous. He will grab at her tail and back with his forepaws and some will even nip the female's rump. Males of some species will mark the fur on the female's back with their sternal (chest) scent gland by grabbing her around the waist from behind and rubbing against her. Some species, e.g. Grey Kangaroos, rub the chest gland against trees and logs, scent-marking their territories.

Among the large kangaroos usually only one male is in close attendance to a female nearing oestrous. Other less dominant males will hang about nearby and make attempts to approach the female, but are chased off by the dominant male as soon as they get too close.

The female will not allow a male to mount her unless she is totally in oestrous. Male kangaroos appear to be more patient than many of the wallabies, calmly following the female around and remaining close by until she is ready for mating. Among the wallabies, often more than one male will be seen relentlessly following the female, sometimes causing her to become quite distressed, especially in warm weather. Female bettongs on the other hand, if not ready to be mated, can become quite violent, lying on their sides, growling and repeatedly kicking at the advancing male.

When copulation does take place the male stands behind the female, grasping her around the waist with his forearms. The length of the mating procedure is variable—it can take five minutes in the Red-necked Wallaby, twenty minutes in the Red Kangaroo and with the Grey Kangaroos up to 40–50 minutes. The mating stance of the female varies between species—some stand, some crouch on all fours with their hindquarters raised, some, like the Rufous Hare-wallaby, lie splayed on the ground with legs and arms spread sideways and the soles of their feet pointing upwards.

The pouch

Female kangaroos have a pouch and males have an external scrotum but no pouch, so it is easy to determine the sex of the animal you are handling.

The pouch in the kangaroo families, unlike that of some other marsupials, is very deep and can almost totally enclose the young up to the stage when it is just about permanently out of the pouch. Female kangaroos have very strong muscle control over the whole of the pouch, especially around the entrance, which can be held so tightly shut that it can be quite difficult to open when you wish to inspect a pouch young. When the female is on the move, especially when hopping, the pouch is held tightly closed so that the joey will not fall out. When the female wishes the joey to exercise she leans forward and, relaxing the pouch completely, uses her forepaws under the pouch to help push the joey out. The female often uses this opportunity to clean the pouch, keeping it relaxed until she is ready for the joey to return. If danger approaches or when the joey is ready to return, she leans forward and tightens the entrance muscle enough to allow it to roll in safely.

Inside a kangaroo's pouch there are two pairs of small teats on the stomach wall at the base of the pouch. The skin inside the pouch is very soft, puffy and moist. In the Red Kangaroo, the teats of each pair are about 1 cm apart and 3 or 4 cm from the other pair. When there is no young in the pouch, there is usually a brown scaly substance and a brown secretion on the skin inside the pouch. The female thoroughly cleans out the pouch during the week before she gives birth.

Birth

About a week before the young is due the female spends a lot of time licking her pouch, in most species sitting on her rump with her back supported and her tail and back legs stretched out in front of her. Some, like the Grey Kangaroo, stand to clean the pouch and give birth, leaning back on the tail with the hind feet pushed forwards.

The newborn young (foetus) measures from 1.5 cm to 2.5 cm in length and ranges in weight from 290 milligrams for the Long-nosed Potoroo to 750 milligrams for the Red Kangaroo; Tammar and Red-necked Wallaby foetuses weigh in at around 460 milligrams. The young can usually be sexed within a few days to three weeks after birth.

An hour or so before the birth, the female intensifies her pouch cleaning, licks her urogenital region and cleans the fur between her cloaca and her pouch entrance. The foetus emerges from the urogenital opening enclosed in an amniotic sac from which it breaks free with its claws about ten to fifteen seconds later. There are no visible external ears or eyes at birth. The foetus is very red in colour at this stage and climbs instinctively and unaided through the fur, using its forearms alternately, for a distance of 15 to 20 cm up the mother's stomach to the pouch entrance. This journey takes about five minutes. The umbilical cord, still attached when it breaks free of the sac, is stretched and broken as the young crawls towards the pouch. The claws that the foetus uses to climb to the pouch are shed soon afterwards and new permanent ones grow. Apparently the foetus always climbs upwards, and on some occasions can actually miss the pouch. Experiments have been conducted where the female has been moved about in different directions and the foetus instinctively changed direction so that it was always climbing upwards regardless of the position of the pouch. We witnessed this once with a Tammar Wallaby, where the foetus had got as far as her chest; by the time we returned with a camera, the foetus was back down at the entrance of

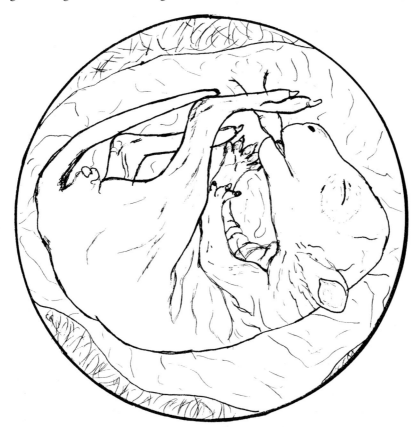

Drawing of a pouch young approximately one-third of the way through pouch life

the pouch. We could not be sure whether the mother had knocked the foetus back with her chin while she was sniffing curiously at it on her chest, or if it had turned around by itself.

Having reached the pouch, the young crawls over the lip of the pouch and takes a few minutes to find one of the teats and attach itself. The teats at this time have developed a small 'bud' on the tip to aid in the attachment of the foetus. One, or even two teats, may be too large for the foetus if there is a young at foot feeding, and another teat may not have shrunk back to a small enough size for the newborn kangaroo. The foetus's mouth at this stage has a large tongue and prominent ridging on its upper palate, presumably to aid in sucking and holding onto the teat, which swells up inside the mouth so that the young is quite firmly attached. The young will stay permanently attached to this teat for about a third to a half of its pouch life. When its mouth is fully open along the sides it can let go of the teat and reattach by itself.

The milk in the teat that the newborn kangaroo is suckling from is of an entirely different composition, lower in fats and protein content, compared to the milk in the teat that the young at foot is drinking from. As the pouch young grows, the milk changes to suit its needs. The milk for the young at foot has a higher fat and protein component, but is reduced in quantity as the young is now eating more vegetation. In other words, each teat has its own 'factory' producing a specific mixture depending on the age of the joey. In good seasons and conditions most kangaroos will have a young in the pouch as well as one at foot, following the mother around and still suckling from the same teat it has drunk from since birth. When the young at foot drinks from the mother's pouch it usually stands in front of her, but sometimes to the side, and often the mother rests her arms on the joey or grooms it while it drinks. After it finishes the mother sometimes grooms her pouch, perhaps cleaning up spilt milk.

With the exception of the Musky Rat-kangaroo which regularly has twins, kangaroos generally have only one young at a time. Twins are known to occur about once in every 500 births, but usually only one survives to the young at foot stage. When twins occur in captivity it is more likely that both will survive as the female has a guaranteed ample food supply and no predators to contend with. Females in captivity have been known to steal another's pouch young and end up raising two.

Bridled Nailtail Wallabies mating in the usual macropod way
(A.P. Dudley)

Tammar Wallaby and Swamp Wallaby having a friendly wrestle, keeping their heads out of the way of each other's claws

Many wallabies, like this Red-necked Wallaby, sit like this while resting or sleeping. This is also the position in which most macropods give birth

A bright red Tammar Wallaby foetus approaching the pouch entrance

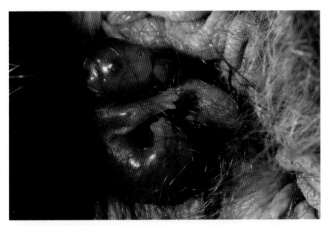

This photo clearly shows the lack of eyes and ears of the newborn foetus, the enlarged nostrils, and the enlarged fore-arms which allow it to climb from the birth canal to the pouch

Female Red Kangaroo and large joey which will drink from its mother until twelve months of age

Post-partum mating

Most macropod species mate again immediately after the birth of a young. A quiescent blastocyst (semi-developed foetus) grows to 0.25 mm in diameter, ceases development and is reserved internally until either the young in the pouch has reached the 'out of the pouch' stage or is lost. This triggers the development of the blastocyst and after the usual gestation period has elapsed, another young is born. In some instances the foetus can be born within 24 hours of the joey leaving the pouch at the normal stage, as the lessened sucking at the teat as the joey grows triggers the embryo's development.

Those species of macropods that do not mate post-partum usually come into oestrous a few weeks or months after the birth and hold a quiescent blastocyst internally until it is required. The only species which appear not to mate until the young has permanently left the pouch are the Western Grey Kangaroo, the Musky Rat-kangaroo and the tree-kangaroos.

Development of pouch young

The joey's life until it reaches independence can be divided into three stages. The first stage, while it is permanently attached to the teat, is total dependence on the pouch for milk and warmth. In the second stage, when it is in and out of the pouch, the joey is not as dependent on the pouch for warmth as it has started thermoregulating itself, but is still quite dependent on the now stronger milk. This major growth stage is preparation for the permanently out of the pouch third stage, when the joey is eating a great deal of solid food and does not rely as much on milk.

Table 3.1 shows when certain physical changes occur during the pouch life of a joey in a selection of macropods. Growth features vary quite considerably between individuals and species.

Table 3.1 Selected growth features during pouch life (days)

Species	Permanently attached to teat	Ears free	Eyes open	Soft fur on head	Fully furred	In & out of pouch
Red-necked Wallaby	–	135	154	–	–	230–275
Agile Wallaby	–	–	126	130	175	190–220
Long-nosed Potoroo	60	93	84–100	90	105	95–125
Spectacled Hare-wallaby	120	–	105	98	–	?–150
Red-legged Pademelon	90–126	105–126	112–126	133–147	–	154–180
Red-necked Pademelon	–	110	110	120	160	?–180
Tasmanian Pademelon	60	100	120	130	160	180–210
Rufous Bettong	87	–	85	87	–	?–114
Tasmanian Bettong	35	85	85	75–85	95	90–105
Little Rock-wallaby	–	85	110	125	–	?–180
Wallaroo/Euro	120	150	140	140	210	210–245
Quokka	60	117	112	125	165	150–170
Red Kangaroo	90	80–90	100–125	130	170	190–240
Grey Kangaroo	130–150	–	170–180	175–201	210	250–300
Tammar Wallaby	100	–	140–150	165–175	195	180–260
Swamp Wallaby	–	–	120–135	150	230	160–260
Parma Wallaby	110	130–150	110	110–150	200–210	?–215

Note: The last number in the 'in & out' column represents the length of pouch life.

Table 3.2 shows pouch life durations, the weaning times in brackets, the sexual maturing times (which vary greatly between individuals and sexes), and breeding season. 'Seasonal breeding' (S) means that mating or births take place only at certain times of the year. 'Not continuous' (NC) means that after the previous young has left the pouch a mating must occur for another young to be born.

Not all species are represented in this table.

Table 3.2 Length of pouch life, maturity and breeding cycles

Species	Pouch life (weeks)	Weaned (weeks)	Sexually mature (months)	Breeding season*
Musky Rat-kangaroo	21	–	12–24	NC
Rufous Bettong	16	22	10–12	C
Tasmanian Bettong	15	23	9–12	C
Burrowing Bettong	17	24	7–14	C
Brush-tailed Bettong	16	19	6–9	C
Northern Bettong	14	–	6	C
Long-footed Potoroo	21	–	24	C
Long-nosed Potoroo	19	21	12	C
Bennett's Tree-kangaroo	36	–	30	NC
Lumholtz's Tree-kangaroo	33	–	–	–
Spectacled Hare-wallaby	21	–	12	C
Rufous Hare-wallaby	18	–	5–18	C
Banded Hare-wallaby	21	39	11–12	C
Agile Wallaby	31	47	12–14	C
Black-striped Wallaby	30	–	14–20	C
Tammar Wallaby	36	39	8–24	S
Western Brush/ Black-gloved Wallaby	28	–	16–22	S
Parma Wallaby	30	–	12–24	C
Whiptail/Pretty-faced Wallaby	39	43	18–24	C
Red-necked Wallaby mainland	39	51	14–19	C
Red-necked/Bennett's Wallaby Tasmania	39	–	14–19	S
Bridled Nailtail Wallaby	19	33	5–10	C
Little Rock-wallaby	26	43	12–24	C
Unadorned Rock-wallaby	29	41	18	C
Brush-tailed Rock-wallaby	29	41	20	C
Yellow-footed Rock-wallaby	28	41	–	–
Tasmanian Pademelon	29	43	14	C
Red-necked Pademelon	26	30	17	C
Red-legged Pademelon	27	–	12–17	C
Quokka	24	34	8–13	S
Swamp Wallaby	34	64	15–18	C
Antilopine Wallaroo	38	54	–	C
Common Wallaroo	35	54	15–24	C
Euro	35	57	18–24	C
Black Wallaroo	–	–	–	S
Eastern Grey Kangaroo	44	77	20–36	C
Western Grey Kangaroo	43	77	20–36	NC
Red Kangaroo	34	51	14–36	C

*S = seasonal, NC = not continuous, C = continuous

Note: Many of these numbers are averages; there is often quite a difference between captive-bred and wild-bred pouch-life development, in addition to natural variations between animals within a species.

· 4 ·

Identification of Macropods State by State

Very young macropods, the age group which most commonly comes into care, are often quite difficult to identify. As they grow, and develop adult coats, the job becomes easier.

In Australia and New Guinea combined sixty-two species of macropods are now recognised, with forty-nine of those species being found in Australia.

We have grouped them together by size and likeness for ease of comparison and identification, in conjunction with State maps. The maps show the general range of each species, but it is not impossible for a species to be found outside these areas. Various factors such as flood and drought can cause animals to move further afield for water or food. In addition, the true distribution of some species is unknown.

We have included drawings of the nose patterns of the three large kangaroos (Red Kangaroos, Grey Kangaroos and Wallaroos) to enable easier identification even of hairless

joeys. The wallabies are much more difficult to tell apart, because many of them have facial and hip stripes and their noses are very similar in shape. If you have a hairless joey, you really need to identify the dead mother if at all possible.

As Queensland possesses the most species of macropods we begin with the identification photos for that state; for the other states we provide photos only of the species that do not appear in Queensland (or any state in between). Where comparison with the species in another state is necessary extra photos are included to help in identification. Photographs of the rock-wallabies are included with their descriptions in Chapter 2, as rock-wallabies are so specific to certain areas they are more easily identified from their distribution; in addition they are not very common road accident victims as they usually do not venture far from their rocky habitats.

Distinctive identifying nose patterns (left to right): Common Wallaroo, Eastern Grey Kangaroo and Red Kangaroo

Spectacled Hare-wallaby showing the distinctive rufous 'spectacles' around the eyes (Sandy Ingleby)

Legend:
- Spectacled Hare-wallaby
- Long-nosed Potoroo
- Musky Rat-kangaroo
- Northern Brush-tailed Bettong
- Rufous Bettong

Musky Rat-kangaroo. This animal has a dark hairless tail and an inner fifth toe (thumb) on its hind foot (Len Robinson/Nature Focus)

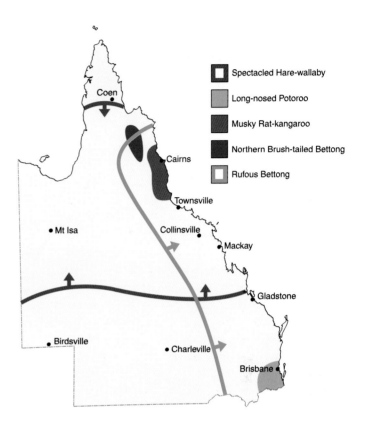

Rufous Bettong (Ian Morris)

Northern Brush-tailed Bettong: This animal is distinct from the Rufous Bettong in that it has a short black brush on its tail and is slimmer in build (Tanya Williams)

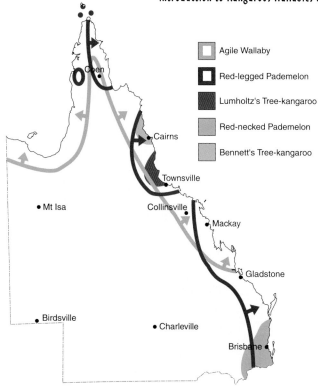

Agile Wallaby
Red-legged Pademelon
Lumholtz's Tree-kangaroo
Red-necked Pademelon
Bennett's Tree-kangaroo

The face of the Bennett's Tree-kangaroo is dark to behind the ears; it has a dark patch on the dorsal surface of the tail just below the rump; the rest of the upper surface of the tail is much lighter than the rest of the tail (Lewis J. Roberts/Nature Focus)

Red-legged Pademelons showing rufous colouration mainly on the hindlegs and forearms and around the face and ears

Red-necked Pademelons usually show rufous colouring only around the neck and shoulders, particularly on the males

Agile Wallaby

Lumholtz's Tree-kangaroo has a dark mask extending from the nose to the forehead (Dave Watts/Nature Focus)

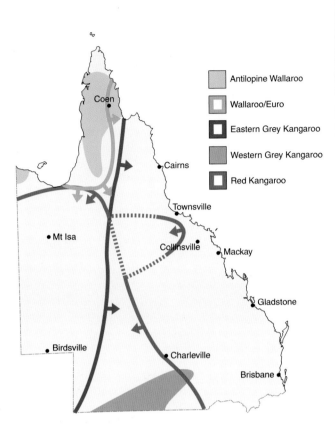

Antilopine Wallaroo

Wallaroo/Euro

Eastern Grey Kangaroo

Western Grey Kangaroo

Red Kangaroo

Eastern Grey Kangaroo

Western Grey Kangaroo—coat is brown in colour with a whitish throat and white tufty fur on the ears

Antilopine Wallaroo

Common Wallaroo/Euro

Red Kangaroos showing the distinctive black and white markings along the side of the muzzle which gives the face a squarish appearance

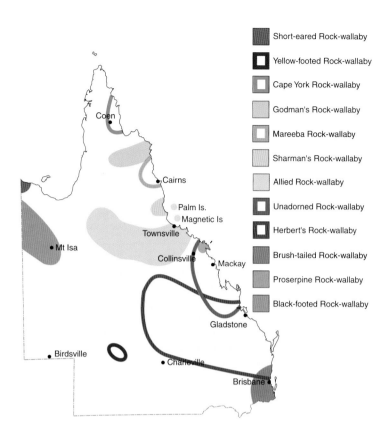

Short-eared Rock-wallaby

Yellow-footed Rock-wallaby

Cape York Rock-wallaby

Godman's Rock-wallaby

Mareeba Rock-wallaby

Sharman's Rock-wallaby

Allied Rock-wallaby

Unadorned Rock-wallaby

Herbert's Rock-wallaby

Brush-tailed Rock-wallaby

Proserpine Rock-wallaby

Black-footed Rock-wallaby

A typical rock-wallaby habitat

Black-footed Rock-wallaby (*Petrogale lateralis purpurecollis*) showing the purple pigmentation on the head and shoulders that is unique to this sub-species

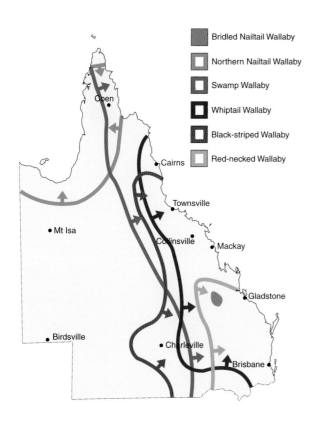

The Northern Nailtail Wallaby is sandy coloured with a dark dorsal stripe down the centre of its back, ending on the tail. They also have a crest of dark hair on the last part of the tail which also has a horny 'fingernail' at the tip (Sandy Ingleby)

Bridled Nailtail Wallaby showing the white stripe that runs from the back of the neck down over the shoulder to behind the forearm. They also have a white hip stripe and a horny 'fingernail' on the tip of the tail (A.P. Dudley)

The Black-striped Wallaby is distinct from the Red-necked Wallaby in that the dorsal stripe goes from between the ears to the centre of the back

Red-necked Wallaby; a young Red-necked Wallaby just beginning to grow fur may appear to have a dorsal stripe like a Black-striped Wallaby until the fur is fully grown

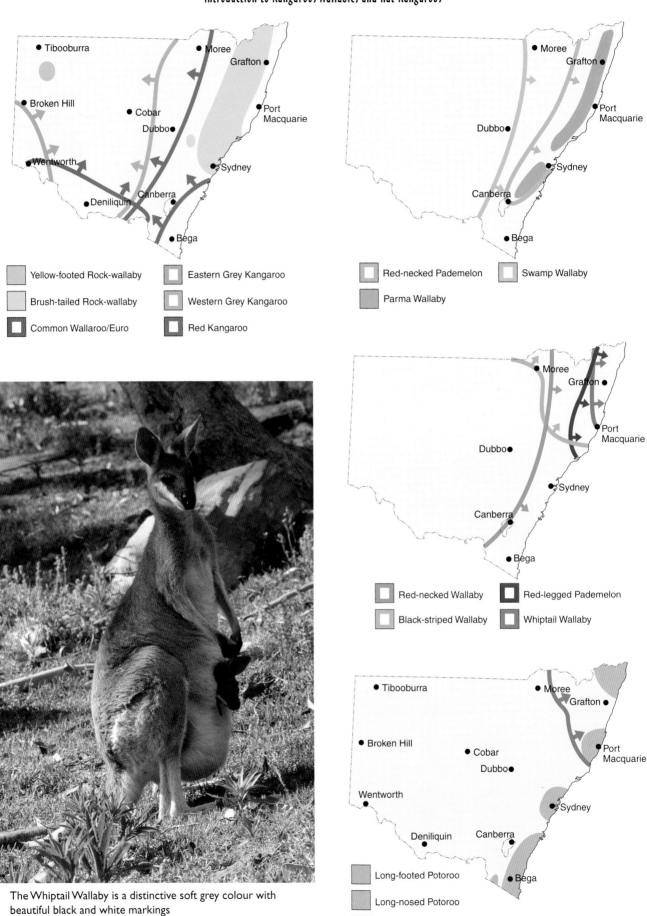

Map 1 (top left) legend:

Yellow-footed Rock-wallaby	Eastern Grey Kangaroo
Brush-tailed Rock-wallaby	Western Grey Kangaroo
Common Wallaroo/Euro	Red Kangaroo

Map 2 (top right) legend:

Red-necked Pademelon	Swamp Wallaby
Parma Wallaby	

Map 3 (middle right) legend:

Red-necked Wallaby	Red-legged Pademelon
Black-striped Wallaby	Whiptail Wallaby

Map 4 (bottom right) legend:

Long-footed Potoroo	
Long-nosed Potoroo	
Rufous Bettong	

The Whiptail Wallaby is a distinctive soft grey colour with beautiful black and white markings

Red-necked Pademelon

The Parma Wallaby is similar in size to the pademelons but has a white throat and chest and a white moustache; many specimens also have a white tip to the tail

The Euro is the inland version of the Common Wallaroo; it is usually a sandy reddish colour which blends in with the sandy colour of its habitat

Red-legged Pademelon

The Swamp Wallaby is quite a dark brown colour with a pale yellow to deep orange front

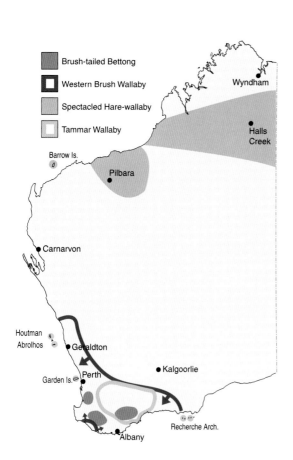

Brush-tailed Bettong

Western Brush Wallaby

Spectacled Hare-wallaby

Tammar Wallaby

Wyndham

Halls Creek

Barrow Is.

Pilbara

Carnarvon

Houtman Abrolhos

Geraldton

Garden Is.

Perth

Kalgoorlie

Recherche Arch.

Albany

Top: Brush-tailed Bettong

Centre: The Western Brush Wallaby has distinctive black hands and feet, black and white ears and a black crest of fur on the last part of its very long tail

Right: The Tammar Wallaby has whitish facial stripes; the males often display a reddish colouration on the forelimbs, hindlimbs and sides

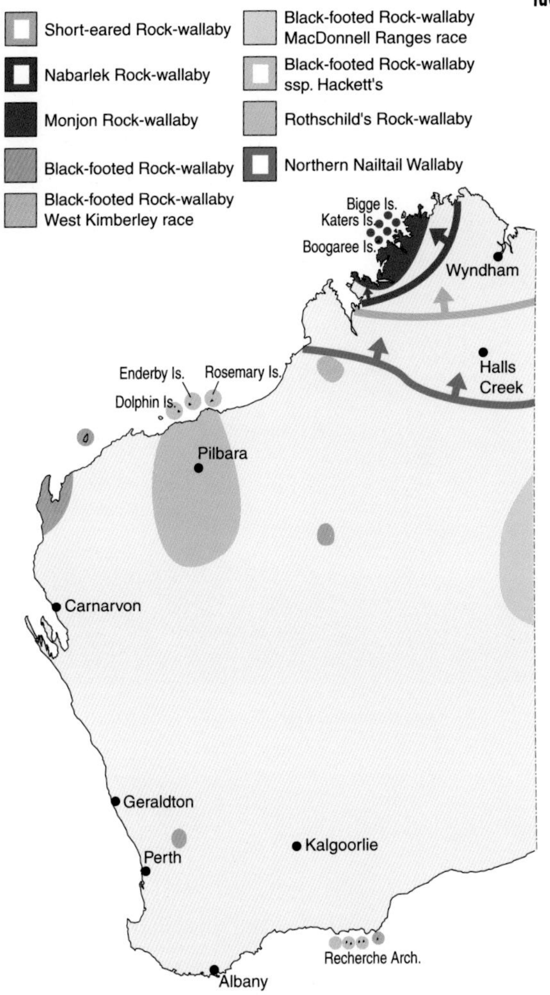

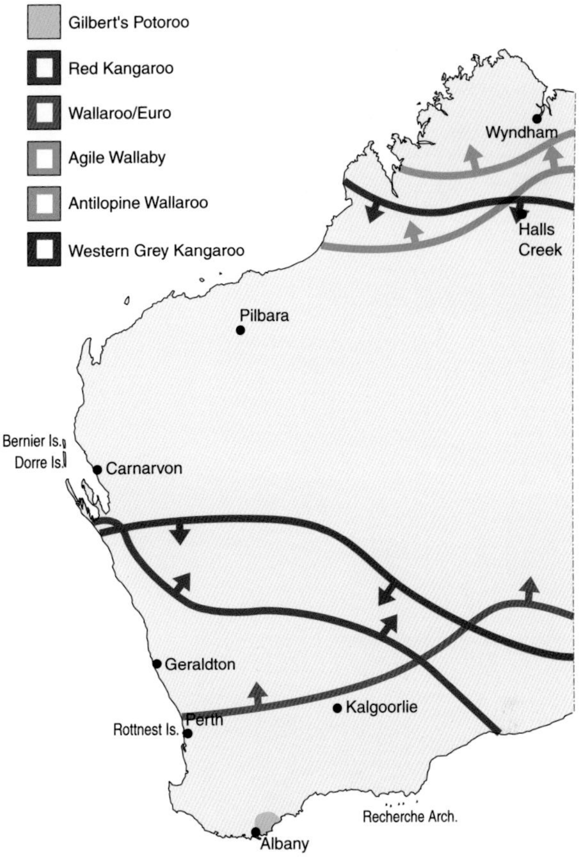

Identification of Macropods

Legend (left group):
- Short-eared Rock-wallaby
- Nabarlek Rock-wallaby
- Monjon Rock-wallaby
- Black-footed Rock-wallaby
- Black-footed Rock-wallaby West Kimberley race
- Black-footed Rock-wallaby MacDonnell Ranges race
- Black-footed Rock-wallaby ssp. Hackett's
- Rothschild's Rock-wallaby
- Northern Nailtail Wallaby

Legend (right group):
- Gilbert's Potoroo
- Red Kangaroo
- Wallaroo/Euro
- Agile Wallaby
- Antilopine Wallaroo
- Western Grey Kangaroo

Left map labels:
Bigge Is., Katers Is., Boogaree Is., Wyndham, Halls Creek, Enderby Is., Rosemary Is., Dolphin Is., Pilbara, Carnarvon, Geraldton, Perth, Kalgoorlie, Recherche Arch., Albany

Right map labels:
Wyndham, Halls Creek, Pilbara, Bernier Is., Dorre Is., Carnarvon, Geraldton, Kalgoorlie, Rottnest Is., Perth, Recherche Arch., Albany

Gilbert's Potoroo

41

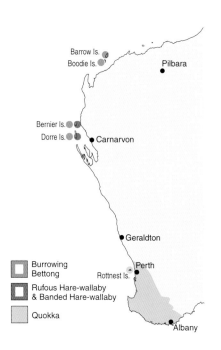

Rufous Hare-wallaby

Burrowing Bettong

Quokkas have no distinguishing markings, but have very short ears and tail and are quite squat in appearance (Arthur White)

Banded Hare-wallaby
(J. & M. Lochman/Nature Focus)

Identification of Macropods

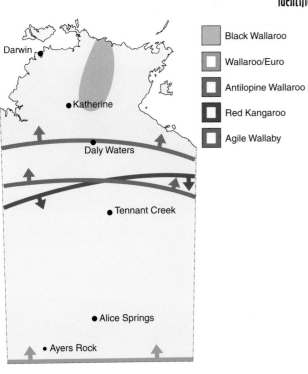

Black Wallaroo

Wallaroo/Euro

Antilopine Wallaroo

Red Kangaroo

Agile Wallaby

Black Wallaroo (Ian Morris)

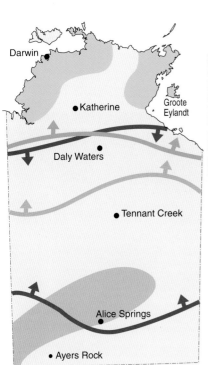

Northern Nailtail Wallaby

Spectacled Hare-wallaby

Black-footed Rock-wallaby

Short-eared Rock-wallaby

Nabarlek Rock-wallaby

Antilopine Wallaroo female with pouch young

Common Wallaroo

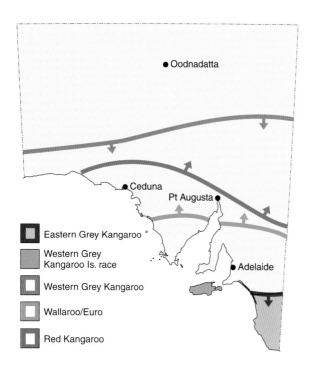

- Oodnadatta
- Ceduna
- Pt Augusta
- Adelaide

Eastern Grey Kangaroo

Western Grey
Kangaroo Is. race

Western Grey Kangaroo

Wallaroo/Euro

Red Kangaroo

Kangaroo Island Western Grey Kangaroo

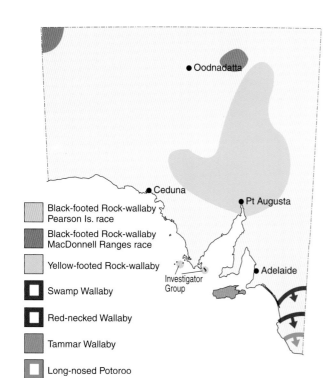

- Oodnadatta
- Ceduna
- Pt Augusta
- Adelaide

Investigator
Group

Black-footed Rock-wallaby
Pearson Is. race

Black-footed Rock-wallaby
MacDonnell Ranges race

Yellow-footed Rock-wallaby

Swamp Wallaby

Red-necked Wallaby

Tammar Wallaby

Long-nosed Potoroo

Black-footed Rock-wallaby, Pearson Island sub-species (Ron Oldfield/Jenny Norman)

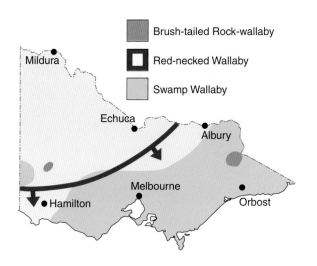

Brush-tailed Rock-wallaby
Red-necked Wallaby
Swamp Wallaby

Long-nosed Potoroo: the most obvious difference between the Long-nosed Potoroo and the Long-footed Potoroo is that the latter's hind foot is longer than its head in animals 100+ days of age, whereas the Long-nosed Potoroo's hind foot is shorter than its head

Wallaroo/Euro
Western Grey Kangaroo
Eastern Grey Kangaroo
Red Kangaroo

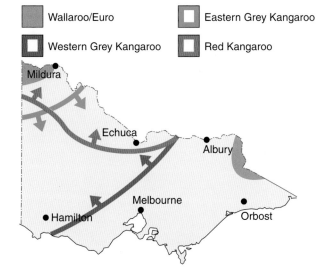

Long-nosed Potoroo
Long-footed Potoroo

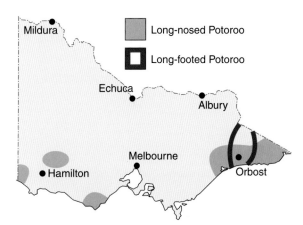

Long-footed Potoroo (Dave Watts/Nature Focus)

Tasmanian Pademelon

Tasmanian Bettong

Red-necked Wallaby (A.P. Dudley)

Eastern Grey Kangaroo (A.P. Dudley)

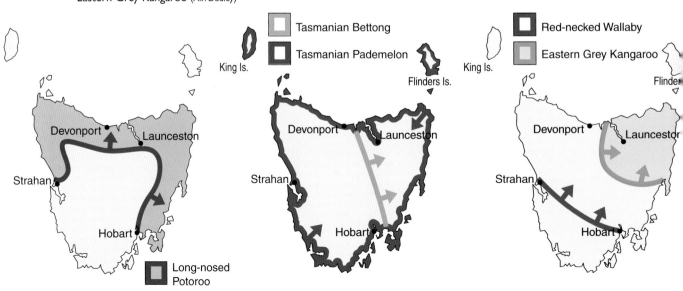

· 5 ·

Physical Features and the Senses

Foot shape and purpose

Foot shape varies between species of kangaroo to cater for different habitats. Among the larger species, the Red Kangaroo and Grey Kangaroo have a narrow foot with only a very small outer toe, whereas the Wallaroo has a broader foot suited to its rocky environment. The long back foot is made up of four toes; the inner fifth toe is no longer present (except in the Musky Rat-kangaroo). The next toe, which is called a syndactylous toe, from a distance looks like one toe but is actually two very small toes encased in a layer of skin with a small split at the end and two claws that are used for grooming. After combing their fur and cleaning out their ears with the syndactylous toe, the kangaroo licks it clean.

The central toe is the large one used when the animals hop; there is also an outer toe which in some species is quite small and insignificant. In some species, such as the Swamp Wallaby and the pademelons, this toe sticks out at about a 60 degree angle from the central large toe, possibly giving the animals more stable footing in the moister habitats that they live in. Rock-wallabies in particular, and Wallaroos, which live among boulders and cliffs, have a much larger central pad on the bottom of the foot with a granulated, soft, non-slip pad which enables them to hop about these rocky areas more easily.

Macropods have five digits on the forelimb, similar to our hands. These digits often have quite long, bluntish claws, and are used for grooming, holding food, grasping food from their lips when it is too long or tough, holding open the pouch and manoeuvring the young while grooming it and

Brush-tailed Bettong demonstrating how the tail is moved to one side to help with balance when the syndactylous grooming claw on the hind foot is used (Tanya Williams)

(above) When kangaroos walk slowly they use forearms, back legs and tail, leaving this imprint (right) in the soil
(Amy Williams)

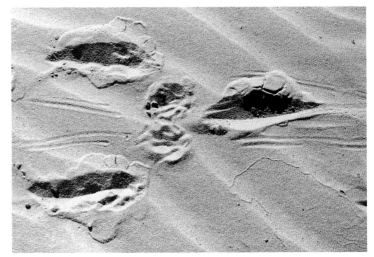

Only about one-third of the macropod's hind foot touches the ground when the animal is hopping. This impression from a Swamp Wallaby's footprint shows the very large outer toe compared with many other macropods for scratching hip-holes in the soil to lie in. They also use their forelimbs for scratching themselves, for holding the females when they are mating and for fighting for supremacy in the group or for possession of a female.

Balancing while grooming is quite a feat, especially when the kangaroo is young. Learning how to position the tail to counterbalance takes quite a bit of practice at times and many joeys end up falling over. Particularly among the longer-legged Red and Grey Kangaroos, it takes quite a while for a joey to realise that the tail has to stay on the ground to form a tripod effect when using the grooming claw on the hind foot to scratch an ear or to comb the fur. Wallabies, whose legs are shorter, seem to be much more co-ordinated than the larger species and also seem to take less time learning to hop efficiently.

The small rat-kangaroos use their long claws to dig burrows or shallow scrapes for nests under bushes, and to collect nesting material. This nesting material, such as grass and bark, is pushed back via the hind feet and transferred to the coiled tail to be carried to a sleeping site to line the nest. Bettongs and hare-wallabies also use their claws to dig for insects, tubers, underground fungi and roots. Many of these small macropods can use their small, strong forelimbs to climb wire fences.

Tree-kangaroos also have softer, more padded soles on their forepaws and hind feet, giving them a better grip when climbing about on slippery tree trunks and branches in the damp climate of tropical Queensland. The feet and legs of tree-kangaroos are more evenly proportioned than those of other kangaroos, being more like those of the Koala—solid limbs with longer claws. They also use their long, thick tails to assist in balancing when moving about high in the rainforest canopy.

Locomotion

Except for the Musky Rat-kangaroo, which has a quadrupedal gait, all macropods hop when they are moving rapidly. When kangaroos hop they place only a very small part of the back foot on the ground and use the tail for balance. The tail does not actually touch the ground, but it does move downwards as the legs move backwards, acting as a counterbalance. A kangaroo's hind feet usually touch the ground less than 10 cm apart (even with the large Red Kangaroo)—if the kangaroo stumbles on uneven ground, the tail is moved sideways to help regain balance.

When the larger macropods walk slowly they use a pentapedal form of movement, utilising hands, feet and tail—the tail and hands are used together to form a tripod as the back legs are moved forward level with the hands. The smaller wallabies, rat-kangaroos, potoroos and bettongs drag their tails behind and very rarely use them for support when walking. When a rat-kangaroo hops the tail is held horizontal

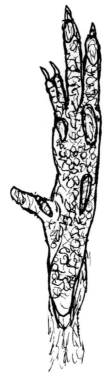

Musky Rat-kangaroo—the only macropod with five toes on the hind foot. They have a thumb which aids them in scrambling up sloping branches and tree trunks

Tree-kangaroo—soft well padded foot for moving along branches

Rock-wallaby—the well-padded granulated foot pad prevents the animal slipping on rocky surfaces. Note the very short claws

Rufous Bettong—foot is very long and thin

The large difference in body size between males and females in many of the macropod species is demonstrated in this pair of Red Kangaroos. The most marked colour difference between males and females is seen in the Red Kangaroo, where the males are reddish and the females blue-grey. The females are popularly known as 'blue flyers' because of their colouring (Tanya Williams)

or higher and the forearms are held very close to the chest, only being used when the animal changes direction or stops. Some species, like the rock-wallabies, Tammar Wallaby and Whiptail Wallaby, hold the arms very rigidly outwards and forwards when hopping, whereas most of the others tuck them close to the chest like the rat-kangaroos.

When a kangaroo increases speed, it is not actually the frequency of the hops that speeds up but rather the length of each stride. They do approximately two hops per second for speeds from 10 kph to 35 kph. The lighter the animal the higher it hops. When a kangaroo wishes to increase speed rapidly it puts in a few short rapid hops and then slows down to a rhythmic gait again.

Tail-swishing

When Swamp Wallabies and Whiptail Wallabies sense danger they swish their tails about on the ground. In common with the larger kangaroos, when they begin to hop away they often thump their feet hard on the ground to warn others of approaching danger. Some male wallabies also demonstrate tail swishing when sniffing a female to see if she is ready for mating.

Sexual differences

Size In the large kangaroos the difference in size between the sexes can be enormous. The male's chest, shoulders and arms become very muscular at maturity; the arms are quite a bit longer in proportion to the body than the female's arms.

Euro in arid habitat showing the sandy coloured coat which aids camouflage

Head of a Western Grey Kangaroo, showing the eyes set on the sides of the head and whiskers protecting the eyes, ears and nostrils, typical of most macropods

Mature females are dwarfed by mature males when they stand side by side. Wallaby males are usually heavier than the females, although in some species this is not quite as obvious as in the larger kangaroos. Among the Hare-wallabies and

the Potoroidae the size difference is even less but the males are usually heavier.

The smallest of the kangaroo family is the Musky Rat-kangaroo which weighs in at 500 g and stands about 20 cm high. Not much larger, but weighing twice as much, is the Long-nosed Potoroo weighing about 1.1 kg. Slightly taller and heavier are the rat-kangaroos which vary from 1.2–3.5 kg; the hare-wallabies which average 1.3–4.5 kg; the Quokka at 2.7–5 kg; and the pademelons which range from 3.8 kg for females up to 12 kg for a large male.

Among the larger wallabies such as the Red-necked, the Black-striped and the Agile, the males can be twice the size of the females, ranging from 4–8 kg in the Bridled Nailtail Wallaby to 9–27 kg in the Agiles. Among the rock-wallabies the males and females are mostly about the same size, ranging from the smallest, the Nabarlek, averaging 1.4 kg, to the largest, the Proserpine, weighing in at 8 kg.

Red Kangaroo males average 66 kg, but can reach 90 kg, whereas female Reds average 26–35 kg; Eastern Greys average 66 kg for males and 32 kg for females; Western Greys are smaller at 54 kg and 28 kg; and Wallaroos weigh around 47 kg and 25 kg. Old stories abounded about 'big reds' which stood '10 feet high', which stretched the truth somewhat. Admittedly a large male red or grey kangaroo standing up on the tips of his toes and tail can look very menacing and can be around two metres high.

Coat colour Besides a marked difference in size between males and females there are many obvious differences in coat colour as well, most notably in the Red Kangaroo, where the male's coat is usually reddish-orange and the female's a lovely blue-grey—they are sometimes called 'blue flyers'. However, individuals are found with opposite coat colours or a mixture of the two. This difference in colour has often meant that males and females were thought to be separate species. The Common Wallaroos also differ in colour—the males being usually a dark grey, almost black, where the females are a soft grey. In the Euros, the inland Wallaroos, the males are often a very deep rust and black mixture, while the females are sandy grey; in the Antilopine Wallaroo the male has a deeper golden colouration than the sandy and grey females.

There is no actual colour difference between the sexes in Grey Kangaroos, but there is a noticeable colour difference between the Eastern and Tasmanian Greys, which are grey, and the Western and Kangaroo Island Greys, which are distinctly brown.

In the wallaby groups, the males quite often have stronger colouration on shoulders or rump, e.g. Red-necked Wallaby males have a deeper reddish colour around the neck and shoulders, sometimes extending partway down their back, than the females.

Hearing, vision, smell and taste

Kangaroos' hearing is quite acute, and they have the added advantage of being able to move the ears independently so they can hear sounds alerting them to danger coming from two directions at once. Kangaroos are normally uneasy on windy days because they cannot pinpoint specific noises around them and because the wind blows away some sounds. On such days, even among the quietest captive stock, it is important that the animals know a human is approaching so that they do not take fright. All it needs is for one to panic and the rest will follow, even when they do not know what the danger is.

The inner part of the ear in the larger macropods has fur growing across the opening, which may prevent insects getting in; this is not found in many of the smaller wallabies. The large ears of the desert dwelling species help dissipate body heat. Kangaroos regularly groom inside their ears using the syndactylous grooming toe.

As a kangaroo's eyes are set wide on the sides of the skull they have only a small area of the landscape in binocular view at any one time but fairly wide monocular lateral vision. This can be demonstrated by walking in a large arc around a kangaroo from a distance of 20 metres or more. Watch the head move jerkily as the animal turns its head to get clear bifocal vision each time you have walked a certain distance. Nonetheless, their eyesight is good and they can recognise dingoes from at least 350 metres away.

The olfactory sense is used in many situations, not just for finding food and water. Macropods greet each other under natural circumstances, and recognise their fostercarers, by sniffing for recognition—you will notice that a kangaroo or wallaby will always stretch forward to sniff you as you approach. The sense of smell is greatly used in their social behaviour. Males pick up the scent markings other males have left when they have rubbed their chest scent glands on branches and vegetation or defecated or urinated on the ground. A male tests a female to see if she is in oestrous by sniffing her cloaca and pouch area and sometimes tasting her urine. The facial action of the male, curling up the top lip while sniffing the female's cloaca, is known as *flehmen*. Flehmen is exhibited by males of many animal species and is thought to help concentrate the smell under the animal's nostrils.

Taste is used to test whether a food is edible or not. Many times an animal will go up to some vegetation, bite into it and instantly let it go, somehow seeming to recognise instinctively that 'this plant is not good to eat'. Young of many animals will sniff or lick their mother's mouths to acquire the smell or taste of different foods. They will often do this to their fostercarers as well, even though they seem to manage quite naturally to judge for themselves what they can eat when they do not have their natural mothers with them.

Vocalisations

Macropods make a great number of different vocal and nasal sounds: hisses, coughs, clucks, distress calls and so on. Clucking sounds made by males when approaching a female are quite soft, almost reassuring noises, perhaps intended to calm her. A male threatening another male who may be trying to approach 'his' female makes clucking sounds much deeper and more threatening. A gruff guttural growl is also made in these confrontations. Wallaroos when startled often give a very loud exhaling hiss just as they begin to hop away; even if you do not actually see the animal or do not get a very clear look you can be fairly sure that it is a wallaroo as it appears to be the only large species to make such a noise.

Soft clucking and clicking or gentle hissing sounds are made by the female when she is calling her pouch young or young at foot to come back to her if danger is approaching. A female Eastern Grey Kangaroo has also been heard to produce a gruff, guttural growl. She had a large pouch young and was approached by her almost independent young at foot. She growled at this older joey as it came near and sniffed at her pouch.

Pouch young and young at foot have a variety of distress calls—some are very loud like the guttural coughing calls made by Grey and Red Kangaroos. Many of the wallabies have a much softer, but high-pitched, hissing call. The Burrowing Bettong has quite a vocabulary of hisses, grunts and squeals, as does the Rufous Bettong. Rufous Bettongs let out a long-drawn hissing call when alarmed; the female will give a low growl when males are checking her for mating and a soft grunt to call her pouch young when it strays too far away. Apparently when a hare-wallaby is alarmed it utters a high-pitched nasal squeak.

Vocalisation has been recorded in pouch young from as early as 50 days in Red Kangaroos, 40 days in bettongs and potoroos and 80 days in the pademelons.

· 6 ·

The Ecology of Macropods

Water consumption

Many macropods feed at night, which means they get moisture from the dew on the grass. Because temperatures are lower at night they do not lose as much body fluid as they would if active during the day. However, most will drink if water is nearby. A few species need to drink regularly in hot weather, like the Red Kangaroos, Euros and Yellow-footed Rock-wallabies. Species which live in rocky areas, like the rock-wallabies and wallaroos, and those which rest underneath thick bushes and shrubbery where it is cooler and away from the radiant heat, still require water, while many of the desert and arid species, under certain conditions, can go without water for a considerable time.

Many of the smaller macropods like the hare-wallabies and bettongs do not appear to require much water at all. Tammar Wallabies have been known to satisfy their thirst by drinking sea-water.

Drinking from creeks and waterholes, a kangaroo or wallaby usually tucks its forearms close to the body and puts its head down to lap the water with the tongue. Even in captivity, drinking from a bowl, they often hold their forepaws out of the way.

It appears from field studies that adult kangaroos will drink about two litres of water during each visit to a water source. Lactating females (feeding large pouch young) require more water than non-lactating animals.

With the increase in dams, bores and other water sources since the arrival of Europeans, some species of macropods, particularly the larger kangaroos, have probably increased their distribution and population sizes.

Effects of drought

Australia's history is marked by the droughts and floods of the country's inconsistent weather patterns; our native animals are often affected by adverse weather conditions.

Red Kangaroos, Eastern and Western Grey Kangaroos and Euros generally range less than 10 km from their home range even during drought times. Even if they did move long distances in drought times they still might not find a better food supply and would use up much-needed fat reserves.

Different species of kangaroos are affected differently, depending on food preferences and conditions. In the 1982–83 drought in Kincheega National Park in western New South Wales about 8900 Western Greys (67 per cent of the Grey population) and 4700 Red Kangaroos (30 per cent of the Red population) died. Of these, most were sub-adults or quite old animals; more males than females died so the surviving males in the population were mainly 3–6 years old. Sixty-four per cent of the animals that died were within 3 km of water, most bodies being found under shady and/or edible trees and shrubs on deep sandy soil. Western Greys died earlier than Reds, but near the end of the three-month summer drought, following a low winter rainfall, the death rate of the Reds was increasing; if the drought had continued the mortality rate of the Reds may have eventually caught up with the Western Greys. During severe droughts, Reds will go to water sources about every four days to drink.

In other drought areas Red Kangaroos have been recorded as moving up to 323 km from their original location, but in Kincheega National Park the Reds moved no more than 9 km and the Western Greys no more than 6 km.

Yellow-footed Rock-wallabies will move up to 5 km to reach water in drought times and Quokkas will increase their home ranges to include waterholes in the hot dry months.

Many female kangaroos carrying pouch young in drought times will lose the larger joey but replace it with the new one waiting in utero—this can happen every couple of months, because as the young grows and starts using the valuable nutrition that the female needs to survive, her milk supply halts, the young dies and yet another one is born. In severe drought, lasting two or three years, the female ceases to come into season at all and the young being held in utero fail to develop; thus no young are produced until better conditions arise. Within two weeks of rain the female comes into season or embryonic development resumes, and breeding continues.

An interesting example of this dependency on water for breeding was seen in studies of Yellow-footed Rock-wallabies in the Flinders Ranges. Where animals were suffering drought conditions with no water source, the females had no pouch young; but less than 2 km away where females had access to a water-well they were carrying pouch young. This phenomenon has also been recorded for the Unadorned Rock-wallaby by Johnson (1979), the Long-nosed Potoroo, Burrowing Bettong, Quokka and Red Kangaroo (Tyndale-Biscoe 1973) and for Eastern and Western Greys (Caughley et al 1984). Another interesting finding was recorded by Chris Allen, who noted that droughts are quite good for the Yellow-footed Rock-wallabies because the dry conditions knock out goats and other competitors. Malnutrition also affects kangaroo populations in drought times.

During drought times more animals tend to be killed on the roadsides where moisture accumulates in the verges and greener grass or vegetation is available to feed on. On a specific 20 km stretch of road in central Victoria, Coulson (1989) recorded the figures shown in Table 6.1 for road-killed Grey Kangaroos and Swamp Wallabies.

Table 6.1 Comparison of road-kills per year

	Grey Kangaroos	Swamp Wallabies
Pre-drought	4.88	1.42
During drought	12.67	4.00
Post-drought	3.64	0.00

Note: Most of these animals were males and nearly half of them were sub-adults.

Thermoregulation

A macropod's normal body temperature is 33°C (92°F). Red Kangaroos living in the arid areas of Australia's interior need to be able to reflect heat as well as be insulated against the freezing temperatures at night in the winter. To cope with these extremes they have a very dense coat that helps to insulate them both against the very cold winter nights (even some summer nights get down to only a few degrees), and the extremely hot dry summer days that regularly reach well over 40°C.

The Red Kangaroo's coat is reasonably light in colour which aids in reflecting the sun's heat. This species has a habit of lying on their backs during the day, with the white fur on their fronts also reflecting heat. In winter the fur grows longer and can change to a deeper, blue colour (especially in the females) which absorbs more heat. If you feel the fur on a sunbaking animal the darker fur feels very warm and the white fur feels cooler.

Red Kangaroos, Euros, Antilopine Wallaroos and Agile Wallabies, which all live in hot summer environments, have white areas on their bodies which are key areas for the cooling process: their forearms, shins and feet, chest and pouch areas. Red Kangaroos lying in the summer sun usually orient themselves to expose the smallest possible area of the body to the sun.

Studies carried out by Dawson and Brown (1970) found that the more reddish coats reflected more solar radiation than the blue, grey-brown or sandy grey coats. Red Kangaroos will sit under shrubs and trees if they are available, but because of the special qualities of their fur they can cope with habitats consisting only of low dense saltbush type vegetation growing to about a metre high. (This can actually provide a better shade cover than taller, less dense shrubs.) When there

A Red Kangaroo swimming to safety from an island of high land where it was trapped during a flood

is very little shade on very hot days, they put their tails between their legs, which cuts down on the amount of exposure to the radiant heat and also restricts the blood flow into the tail area.

When macropods become overheated or stressed they pant. This is their major form of heat dissipation. They also lick the forearms and the shin area of the hindlegs where there are networks of blood vessels close to the skin surface, so that as the blood flows through these areas it is cooled by the saliva-dampened skin—this is called evaporative cooling. The blood is pumped more rapidly through these areas causing the body's temperature to return to normal quite rapidly. Other areas licked are the chest, the outside of the pouch, and the scrotum. A female with pouch young will lick the outside of the pouch to help maintain a constant temperature for the joey, usually around 32°C (90°F). The large ears of most kangaroo species found in deserts and other hot dry areas also aid in heat loss, especially if the animals are active during the day.

Species like the Western and Central Euros, living in hot arid areas, which have less dense, shaggy, dark-coloured coats, need to seek shelter in rocky outcrops, caves and well-vegetated gullies to escape daytime heat and radiation. Their coat colour is more useful for camouflage than for heat deflection. Animals like the Grey Kangaroos, with dark-coloured coats, usually live in wooded areas where they can seek shade in the hot weather.

Some species, like the nocturnal Burrowing Bettong, go down into burrows where the temperature rarely exceeds 30°C (86°F) no matter what the above-ground temperature reaches. Animals like the Spectacled Hare-wallaby sleep in forms or depressions within porcupine grass clumps where the temperature reaches only 32–34°C (90–94°F) even when the outside reading may be as high as 50°C (122°F).

Swamp Wallabies in captivity have been seen to dangle their arms in water troughs to cool down, or walk through standing water if it is not too deep. As their name implies, they do not mind living in damp areas anyway. With the exception of Swamp Wallabies, macropods in general do not like water and when it rains heavily for too long they start to look quite miserable. Rock-wallabies especially do not like rain. They will not even leave the rock pile if it rains all night; if they happen to be out feeding away from their shelter they will stand under trees, returning to the rocks if the rain persists.

There are occasions when the weather gets hot enough to persuade kangaroos to like water. Grey Kangaroos in coastal areas have been seen paddling along the beaches. Near Broken Hill in the middle of summer we once saw a Red Kangaroo standing under a spray of water coming from a broken pipe. A young Grey joey we were rehabilitating years ago in the Lightning Ridge area used to hop into a shallow 5 cm deep paddling pool when the outside temperature reached about 42°C (108°F).

Kangaroos can and will swim if they have to—usually only when they become trapped in flooded areas and have to swim to dry land. When they swim their legs move alternately and independently. Unfortunately, pouch young generally drown if a female has to swim far; fully enclosed joeys have been known to survive where the mother has only to swim a few metres.

Grazing patterns

Grazing refers to the time that an animal spends actively eating. Southwell (1981) recorded Eastern Grey Kangaroos grazing an average of 17 hours a day in autumn and winter and 15 hours in spring and summer. Red Kangaroos graze for 7–10.5 hours a day in all seasons, Western Grey Kangaroos for 5.9–10 hours daily, mostly at night, particularly just after sunset, in the early morning and during sunrise. Western Grey Kangaroos ate for less time in summer when food was more abundant. Males of all species, in general, eat for one hour longer than females.

In the wild or where there is an available mixture of grasses and shrubbery, macropods will go for the nitrogen-rich species. In the summer months when the shrubs are higher in nitrogen, animals like Swamp Wallabies become browsers rather than grazers.

Gregariousness

It is usually the larger and middle-sized macropods that move around in groups, with the exception of the Wallaroo, Red-necked Wallaby and the Swamp Wallaby. Eastern and Western Grey Kangaroos most commonly group together—anything from 3 to 16 individuals for the Westerns and up to 23+ for the Easterns. The Antilopine Wallaroo, Red Kangaroo, Whiptail, Agile and Black-striped Wallabies are known to mass into groups of 10+ members. Rock-wallabies appear to live in groups, but this is probably because of the limited size of their specific habitats. Other wallabies use communal feeding areas, especially when the grazing area is adjacent to a forest populated by a mixture of pademelons and wallabies. When they have finished feeding or are disturbed, they disperse as individuals.

Home ranges

Home ranges are areas of habitat that an animal uses over a number of months for foraging, breeding and resting. The size of these areas can vary, depending on the social organisation of a species and often on seasonal and weather conditions, whether feed is abundant close to their normal home ground or whether drought means they must range further to find food and water. In some species there is a difference in home range sizes between males and females.

During the sixteen months from July 1979 to November 1980, 261 Red Kangaroos and 170 Western Grey Kangaroos were caught and tagged during studies in western New South Wales (Denny 1980). Over the following seven years, analysis of 1751 recorded sightings revealed that kangaroos tended to stay within the same area for many years. Only 18 per cent of the kangaroos tagged moved more than 10 km from where they were caught, but two animals were recorded moving long distances. These were both Red Kangaroos that moved during drought, one having travelled 216 km; the other, a female tagged in Kinchega National Park in May 1980 and recorded 2 km away in December 1981, turned up an amazing 323 km away near Lake Frome in January 1986, where she was unfortunately shot. The longest recorded movement so far for a Western Grey is only 85 km.

In another study, three out of four Red Kangaroos caught and tagged, then released up to 20 km from their place of capture, found their way back to their original home ground. Two were back within ten weeks of being moved, the third within a year; all three subsequently stayed in those areas for at least the next eighteen months. The fourth, which originally headed in the right direction, did not find its way back, appearing to become confused by a long dog-leg in a fence that barred its way (Priddel et al 1988).

Table 6.2 shows a cross-section of macropod home ranges, starting with the smaller species. Home ranges do not necessarily increase in size with the size of the animal. Some of the small rat-kangaroos and wallabies will travel up to 2 km a night from their sleeping area to find feeding areas. Much depends on food sources and shelter, type of food, e.g. the availability of fungi for potoroos and rat-kangaroos, and habitat preferences, e.g. rocky areas for rock-wallabies who do not like to stray far from their refuges.

Life span

Life expectancy in macropods varies from 8 to 27 years. Kangaroos can be aged by molar eruption, by the number of molars left in their jaws and by the amount they are worn down.

The average life expectancy of Red and Grey Kangaroos in the wild is approximately 15–18 years, although some tagged Red Kangaroos have been recorded at 20 years of age, and even more exceptional ones at 24 to 27 years in the wild. Usually by the time they are in their late teens their molars have moved forward and shed and they only have a couple left to chew with, so that it becomes difficult for them to eat tough grasses. A Red Kangaroo caught and marked 274 km north of Broken Hill in 1964 when it was about 2 years old was shot in early 1990 in poor condition on a station south of the Barrier Highway near the New South Wales/ South Australia border. This animal was 27 years old and had moved 300 km as the crow flies (Bailey et al 1992).

One exception to the rule of tooth movement occurs in the Nabarlek Rock-wallaby, which continuously grows molars that move forward and shed throughout its life, enabling the animal to cope with a diet of vegetation which can contain up to 40 per cent silica inclusions (phytoliths) which causes constant wear on teeth.

In general, wallabies and rat-kangaroos reach between ten and fifteen years of age; e.g. the Long-nosed Potoroo can live up to twelve years, during which time a female can produce from ten to fifteen offspring. Conditions such as drought and heavy predation obviously reduce life span averages.

Declining macropod populations

Competition from herbivores There are quite a few reasons for the disappearance and the decline of some species of macropods, and for the increase in populations of others. One of the major problems is the spread of the millions of grazing domestic sheep and cattle throughout large areas of Australia, competing for often scarce vegetation and trampling the soil. The destruction of habitat means many species become more vulnerable to predation by feral and native predators; habitat destruction also leads to the isolation of colonies with the associated threat of inbreeding, and can eventually lead to extinction of a species once any remaining suitable habitat is destroyed. The plight of the Bridled Nailtail Wallaby, near Dingo in Queensland, is an example. These animals rely for cover on the Brigalow Scrub, largely destroyed through extensive clearing for agriculture. One of the last remaining areas of this habitat has now been reserved solely for their survival. Valuable habitats for some of the smaller macropods, like the Rufous Bettong, the Long-nosed Potoroo and the Red-legged Pademelon, have been removed by the loss of the Big Scrub on the New South Wales north coast, and much of the Illawarra Scrubs through development.

Europeans introduced a variety of animals to Australia which eventually became feral. Between 1788 and 1859 eighteen attempts were made to establish rabbits in the wild. Finally (unfortunately) the rabbit spread successfully over most of Australia, except into the tropical areas of the north. Hares, originally released for hunting (some also escaped from greyhound-coursing establishments), now live along the coast and ranges from central Queensland through to Victoria and south-eastern South Australia. Their impact on the environment is not as devastating as that of rabbits because they do not construct burrows and population numbers are generally low.

Goats are able to survive in semi-arid and arid pastoral areas but do require drinking water during dry spells; thus they tend to be found in sheep-grazing areas where water is usually available. Some of the worst damage that goats do is to the vegetation—what the rabbits don't eat as seedlings the goats eat as young bushes. Eventually they can eliminate

Table 6.2 Home ranges in hectares

Species	Females	Males
Tasmanian Bettong	65–135	65–135
Rufous Bettong	45–60	75–110
Allied Rock-wallaby (wet season)	8.8 (core area 2.7*)	8.8
(dry season)	16.1 (core area 5.5*)	16.1
Brush-tailed Rock-wallaby	15.2	15.2
Yellow-footed Rock-wallaby	both sexes 150–200 in rocky areas	
Spectacled Hare-wallaby	8–10	8–10
Bridled Nailtail Wallaby	26–40	59–90
Bennett's Tree-kangaroo	up to 25	up to 25
Red-legged Pademelon	1–4	1–4
Tasmanian Red-bellied Pademelon	170	170
Black-striped Wallaby	91	91–192
Swamp Wallaby (16 ha. average)	14–86	14–91
Whiptail Wallaby	65.8	65.8
Red-necked Wallaby (15.2 ha. average)	11.8	31.6
Western Grey Kangaroo (50 ha. average)	39–70	39–70
Western Grey in Hattah Kulkyne (3 or 4 habitats in home range)	220–460	220–460
Eastern Grey Kangaroo	20–23	20–23
Wallaroos	85 (core area 25*)	220–300 (core area 65–85*)
Euros (summer)	30	77
(winter)	27	30

* Core area refers to the area in which the animal spends the majority of its time grazing and resting.

certain plant species, as the plants never reach maturity to flower and produce seeds and so regenerate. Goats have been quite devastating for the rock-wallabies because they take over their caves and rocky outcrops and eat their food resources. The one thing that does help slightly is that goats need to drink very regularly and thus require a permanent water source, whereas the rock-wallabies can withstand a certain period without water.

Feral horses survive patchily over Australia, but not usually in the desert areas. Camel and donkey populations, derived from escapees from expeditions by early explorers and traders, have spread into the desert areas not favoured by horses, and patchily into other areas of the inland.

Pigs are omnivorous (carnivorous as well as herbivorous) and are found over most of Queensland and New South Wales, in the tropical north of the Northern Territory and patchily in the very north and the extreme south-west corner of Western Australia. They are very competitive with native animals in a variety of habitats, especially in rainforests.

Predation from carnivores Carnivorous feral animals have caused havoc in the Australian environment, where they seem to thrive. The cat appears to have arrived even before European settlement in the late 1700s. It has been suggested

that the early Dutch explorers left cats behind in Western Australia two hundred years earlier. Cats have played a big part (and still do) in the elimination of many of our native mammal species. They have established themselves Australia-wide, from thick forests to the driest desert areas, feeding on probably anything that moves; they are very efficient predators, and can kill small macropods up to two kilograms in weight along with birds, native mice and so on.

The dingo, a large carnivore, arrived in Australia sometime around 4000 years ago and may have been the reason that the Thylacine became extinct, through food competition, on mainland Australia. The dingo has established itself, now mainly as cross-breeds with feral domestic dogs, in various habitats throughout Australia and on some offshore islands, except for Tasmania.

When Eastern Grey Kangaroos in the wild are approached by dingoes they usually become alert and flee. They may run from a dingo 350 metres away, but usually don't react until the dingo is within 200 metres. Large males will sometimes go to water or fight them off (one was recorded fighting off a dog for over 63 minutes). On a property near Narran Lakes in New South Wales we saw a large male Grey Kangaroo being chased by a dog, retreat to the water where the lake came in under a fence. It stood in the water with its back to the fence, waiting to grab the dog if it came close enough. Dogs are known to have been drowned by kangaroos in this situation.

In the larger species many animals weighing 20 kg or less are taken by dingoes and feral dogs. Most wallabies weigh less than that so are easy prey. Swamp Wallabies are a main prey of dingoes in the forests of eastern Australia, especially the young. Females carrying young, up to 14–25 per cent of their weight, have trouble getting up enough speed to escape. They are likely to drop the young out of the pouch in their efforts to get away.

Foxes, released in the 1860s for sporting practices, have also played a major part in the decline of our native animals over most of Australia, except for the tropical north. Fortunately, it appears that the rabbit is also an important source of food for the fox—where foxes have been eliminated the rabbits have multiplied. An unfortunate consequence of the release of the rabbit Calicivirus is likely to be increased predation by foxes on our native fauna. Studies have shown that foxes have a major impact on some species that are already endangered, e.g. rock-wallabies, bettongs and hare-wallabies.

Some people say they 'shoot kangaroos for sport', others shoot large males to feed their dogs, while kangaroos are also culled commercially for their meat and fur because they overgraze areas of pastoral and agricultural lands. Many macropods, large and small, suffer from the effects of increasing traffic, being killed and injured on our roads.

Not all predators are feral or human. Native predators like Tiger Quolls, Tasmanian Devils, Chuditch (Western Native Cat), Wedge-tailed Eagles, White-breasted Sea-eagles, large pythons, goannas and owls, prey upon the smaller macropods like the rat-kangaroos. Many of these predators also scavenge road-killed macropods.

We have witnessed a Wedge-tailed Eagle dive-bombing a Euro female and young at foot on a rocky outcrop, presumably in the hope that one would stumble and be injured or die to provide the eagle's next meal (these animals were too large for the eagle to grab and carry off). This behaviour has also been reported against rock-wallabies. Rabbits are regularly captured by eagles and have probably contributed to the increase in Wedge-tailed Eagle numbers, especially since the eagle has benefited from protection by law and more enlightened attitudes among land-owners. The lowering of rabbit numbers from the Calicivirus may lead to increased predation by eagles on native species or, conversely, a decline in eagle numbers.

Altered fire regimes In times past many macropods benefited from Aboriginal fire-stick farming techniques (regular low slow burns). This style of burning has been going on for over 40 000 years, time enough for many animals to become dependent on the routine. The Rufous Hare-wallaby is one macropod that prefers fresh tips of vegetation as the main part of its diet. Modifications to fire regimes since European settlement are suggested as the cause of declines in some species, especially in the semi-arid areas and the tropical north.

This Eastern Grey Kangaroo being chased by a dog ran to the water, put its back against the fence and braced itself, ready and waiting for the dog to approach. Sometimes kangaroos will stand in water halfway up their bodies

PART II

HAND-RAISING MACROPODS

· 7 ·

When a Joey Comes Into Care

Hand-raising macropods (or any other native animal, for that matter) is not a simple pastime. It is a constant, tiring and sometimes upsetting task, especially if an orphan dies or becomes very ill after you have spent hours, days or weeks battling for its survival, but a very rewarding task when you win and the animal survives. It is even better when you experience the satisfaction of finally releasing a healthy animal into its natural environment to continue the cycle of life. These young animals provide many hours of enjoyment and interesting experiences with their habits and playful antics. When you have had the chance to watch them in the wild or in family groups, it is interesting to recognise their natural instincts coming to the fore while you are raising them.

The task of hand-raising is not to be taken lightly as it involves many interrupted, even sleepless, nights. If you have to go out visiting or go away on holidays you have to arrange for your little orphan to be 'babysat' or cared for just as you would a human baby. These problems have to be addressed before you take on the responsibility of fostering native fauna. Even after twenty-seven years of hand-raising orphan kangaroos, possums, bandicoots and birds we find it is still a task that keeps us on our toes, because no orphan that comes in requires exactly the same conditions as the previous one.

It's not easy!

A hairless male Agile Wallaby (nearly four months old), 'looked after' by an inexperienced person for four days before it came to us, had been kept too hot on top of a heater, had fallen onto the heater and been burned down one side of its body. I kept it next to my skin, day and night, for one and a half weeks, injecting fluid under the skin at regular intervals (under veterinary advice regarding the quantity required), feeding it every 1½ to 2 hours, day and night. Finally the little wallaby settled into a routine of drinking a suitable amount at each feed, his body rehydrated and he recovered from his ordeal. From this unpromising start a very sturdy healthy adult was successfully released into a group of Agile Wallabies in a wildlife park.

Another case demonstrating the enormous input of time and effort required in fostercaring was that of a five-month-old hairless female Red Kangaroo found abandoned after a day of heavy rain. With soil in her eyes and ears, and abrasions down one side of her body from scrabbling on the ground, she was very cold and unresponsive to stimuli. Cleaned and warmed and kept next to my skin most of the night, by six in the morning she was still unresponsive and a candidate for euthanasia. Three hours later, out of the blue she started to drink. Three days later you would not have believed it was the same animal.

She progressed rapidly until she grew a short coat of fur and started to move around, when she kept bumping into objects and we realised she was blind. Again euthanasia looked like the only option. Veterinary examination revealed no obvious problem. Three or four days later she was able to see again, so once more she had eluded the end.

A few weeks later, however, her ankles started swelling and she had difficulty walking and hopping. An infection which had apparently lain dormant since her initial accident flared up when she became active on rough ground. Eventually, the bacterium responsible was isolated and treated, and the (by now expensive) kangaroo was successfully assimilated with a captive group.

Of course, not all orphans come to you in such parlous condition, but remember—a baby is a baby, whether human or animal.

Protected animals—yes and no!

The need for a permit to care for native Australian animals on your premises varies between states; in many states you are required to have a National Parks & Wildlife Licence. In New South Wales, South Australia, the Northern Territory, Queensland and Tasmania permits should be applied for as soon as possible after you acquire the animal. In New South Wales permits are usually given only to people who are members of a recognised wildlife rescue organisation. In all cases an animal must be released, through the proper organisations, as soon as its behaviour indicates an ability to survive on its own. An animal raised alone will need to be assimilated with others of its own species before release.

In Victoria there are at least 150 wildlife shelters to which an injured, sick or orphaned animal should be taken, as permits are not issued to unauthorised carers. To contact a shelter call the Conservation, Forests and Lands Department on (03) 9450 8600. The same situation applies in the ACT—native fauna should be handed over as quickly as possible to the Wildlife Foundation ACT Inc. (02) 6296 3114.

The only state that does not require you to have a permit is Western Australia, but the animal must be sick, injured or orphaned to be in care; once it has reached a sufficient age or state of health to be released arrangements must be made with the Department of Conservation and Land Management (08) 9367 0436.

Names, addresses and phone numbers of wildlife authorities for all states are listed in Appendix C (page 102).

Why joeys are orphaned

There are many reasons why fostercarers end up with an orphaned joey to raise. Most of their mothers have died on the roads, others have been killed by weekend shooters, others by cat and dog attacks; some orphans even come from captive colonies, where sometimes a mother abandons its young or becomes ill or dies.

Many fostercarers begin their fostering role faced with one of the above predicaments. If you wish to become a carer there are many organisations that you can join. Many groups organise training classes to teach the necessary skills for rescuing and caring for native animals. The more you can learn about kangaroos and wallabies, the easier it is to understand their many habits when you are caring for them. Names and addresses are listed in Appendix D on page 103; contact them for advice.

The aim of fostering

The aim of fostering a native animal is to raise it and ultimately prepare it for release back into its natural habitat. Unfortunately this ideal is not always realised.

Some joeys are kept illegally as pets by their finders until they are fully grown, when they are found to become a problem (especially males); alternative accommodation then has to be found. Some of these joeys are just released into the wild, on occasions well outside their natural distribution, to 'survive' on their own; such 'pets' often come to a traumatic end. This should not happen. If you are to be a fostercarer you must always have the animal's welfare and future in the wild as your main objective.

It is usually better to have more than one joey at a time, because two or more joeys together, approximately the same age, form a relationship which means they do not require non-joey company as much. They do not have to be of the same species for this to happen. This companionship is very valuable when they are moved to new quarters or a new area for further rehabilitation prior to release into the wild. They seem to settle into this new environment much more quickly and in a more relaxed manner. Young at foot being prepared for final release need to be assimilated with their own species to form a peer group. With luck such a group stays together until the animals settle into their final environment.

The Agile Wallaby that survived all the mishaps recounted on page 61 developed into a strong healthy adult

Three Swamp Wallabies approximately five, six and seven months old. The fur is just beginning to show as a grey patch on the top of the youngest one's head. The fur grows first on the head, the part that usually sticks out of the pouch first (Dennis Browning)

Eastern Grey Kangaroo joey with plastered foreleg after it was caught in a fence

Dealing with a new orphan

Many joeys come from the pouches of female macropods that have been killed by cars. A joey can survive in the pouch of a dead female, sometimes for up to two or three days, depending on the environmental temperatures at the time.

First twenty-four hours of care In an emergency, if you do not have a bag or cloth to wrap the newly-orphaned joey to calm and warm it, the next best thing is to put it inside your shirt or even wrap it in your skirt. Unfurred or just-furred joeys are often cold (if the mother has been dead for some time), as they are unable to maintain their body temperature. They must be placed next to a heat source (your skin in an emergency) to regain a normal temperature. The older the joey, the more stressed it is likely to be and the longer it will take to settle in. If the mother is not dead, she will probably be so badly injured that she will need to be euthanased. The animal should be wrapped in a blanket and taken to the nearest veterinarian as soon as possible. (Euthanasia by the roadside by an unqualified person is unlikely to result in prosecution.)

As soon as possible, wrap the orphan snugly in a flannelette pillowcase and woollen jumpers and keep it warm and quiet. A rescuer not intending to raise the joey should not attempt to feed it but should take it to a fostercarer or veterinarian who will pass it on to a recognised organisation as soon as possible. If you cannot deliver the animal to a qualified carer within a few hours, feeding it a solution of glucose and warm water (see page 77) may be necessary.

Unfortunately, unqualified people who find a joey sometimes attempt, with the best of intentions, to raise it themselves; in many cases their inexperience leads to a very sick orphan which is eventually passed on to a qualified carer or veterinarian. This makes the job of successfully rearing the animal much harder.

Holding a joey Very small pouch young should be cradled in your hands. They should not be picked up around the ribs without being supported under the tail and back legs as this makes them feel very insecure and may result in spinal injuries. The best way to hold larger animals is to grasp the base of the tail with one hand while placing your other hand around the front of the chest, under its forearms, then cradling the animal while still holding the base of the tail.

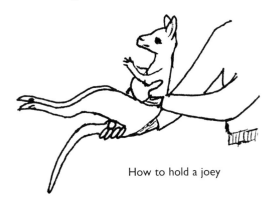

How to hold a joey

Assessing the joey's condition

When a new joey arrives it must be checked thoroughly for any injuries which might make it a candidate for euthanasia. Bruising or internal bleeding is more easily seen on hairless joeys, but on furred animals it is often not possible to detect this type of injury, especially likely to occur in road accident victims.

If a joey has to be cleaned, do it gently with warm water, then dry the animal and wrap it warmly. A quiet hairdryer can be used to help dry and warm a furred joey, but make sure it is not too hot. Hardened faeces and dirt can also be cleaned off young animals using moist towelettes, e.g. Wet Ones. They seem to dissolve the dirt more quickly than water, and the other benefit is that the animal does not get as wet or cold. Be careful, however, to avoid using them near the joey's eyes.

If you feel that the joey needs veterinary attention, either for treatment of injuries or euthanasia, take it to the surgery as soon as possible to prevent any prolonged suffering. If you intend to raise the joey, whether its injuries are minor or special care is required, you must decide quickly whether you have the time and the ability to care for it correctly or whether you should hand it over to a more experienced carer. If you decide to look after the joey yourself you must be prepared to hand it over to the appropriate authorities when it is old enough, so that it may be released back into the wild correctly with others of its own species.

Hairless joeys with their eyes closed, their ears still flat to their heads and their mouths still partially sealed are very difficult to raise, especially if you have not had any previous experience. It is very time-consuming and rewarding when you do succeed with animals this size, but more often they are very difficult, even heartbreaking, to rear. A hairless joey is more difficult to raise than a furred one because of heat and moisture loss, less ability to suck, and so on, but devoted carers have raised many such joeys to become healthy breeding animals.

If the joey's eyes are open, the animal is almost at the stage where the soft fur will come through, and hand-raising is more likely to be successful. The task of hand-raising well-furred joeys is made easier by the fact that they can more readily maintain their own temperature, although they will still need some form of extra heating in very cold weather. If you can spend the time on a little orphan then try, otherwise it is better to pass it on to an experienced fostercarer or have it euthanased.

Often, even in road-kill situations, the joey is physically uninjured but dehydrated, depending on the length of time the mother has been dead and/or the weather conditions. In hairless joeys that might have been lying out of the pouch for a few hours, dehydration is likely in combination with sunburn, windburn or pneumonia.

Common ailments

Burns If an animal has been caught in a bushfire or burnt in any way, simply apply clean damp cloths to the affected areas and take it to a veterinarian as soon as possible. Keep the cloths damp to prevent them sticking to the burnt area and to keep the wound cool. The animal may be dehydrated so offer (or administer) a solution of glucose and water, Lectade or a similar solution.

Shock An animal in shock is best kept in a quiet, dark, warm area. Offer an oral fluid of 5–10 g glucose per 100 ml warm boiled water. This can be administered very carefully with an eye-dropper or, if the animal is capable of lapping, offered in a shallow dish, being careful to support the head so the animal does not immerse its nose while drinking.

Injuries An injured animal should be placed carefully on its side on a level surface, making sure that the head is not pushed down onto the chest or pushed back so far as to restrict breathing. This position allows any build-up of saliva, blood, etc. to drain from the animal's mouth so it does not choke. Put a towel or similar under its head to absorb any such liquids and prevent the animal's fur becoming wet. If there is excessive bleeding from an injury, a pressure bandage or tourniquet should be applied in the appropriate position. Handle the animal as little as possible to avoid stressing it more or further aggravating any injuries (there may be internal injuries that you do not know about). Cover the animal or wrap it in a warm cloth or blanket, keeping it warm but not too hot (refer to page 72, 'Maintaining body temperature') and take it to a veterinarian as soon as possible.

Dehydration Dehydration can be tested for by pinching the skin on the animal's back. Skin which does not smooth out again reasonably quickly indicates dehydration. If the dehydration is only minor, and the joey begins drinking well fairly quickly, the administration of electrolyte replacers may not be necessary. More serious dehydration requires immediate attention. An electrolyte replacer such as Lectade or Vitrate is usually mixed with warm water and bottle-fed or very carefully syringe-fed orally. (Sometimes administering such fluids is more stressful than the problem itself, so judgment is required.) In severe cases subcutaneous administration of fluids may be required under veterinary care.

Stress All newly acquired macropods are likely to be suffering from stress. Stress can be very hard to determine in some animals—they show it in many different ways. Some become very quiet, others race about like lunatics, others develop diarrhoea, others don't feed properly, all of which can leave them vulnerable to disease. If the stress reaction lasts more than a day or two a veterinarian should be consulted.

Usually an animal that is feeding well and still looking healthy after seven days has an excellent chance of surviving

Six-and-a-half month old Common Wallaroo joey (Dennis Browning)

to release stage. On average it takes about this time for a joey's stomach to settle to the changeover in milk and artificial conditions.

Diarrhoea Diarrhoea, particularly in newly acquired animals, is often a result of stress or dietary problems. One sign that a macropod is suffering from a stomach disorder is when their bodies contort in spasms and their legs cave-in towards their stomachs. If an animal has diarrhoea for more than two or three days, sooner if the motions are particularly dark and offensive, the faeces should be checked for bacteria or parasites, e.g. coccidiosis, salmonella or worm infestations. For some of these to show up in tests, samples of droppings from three days in a row need to be tested.

Intestinal infections Candidiasis (thrush), caused by the yeast *Candida albicans*, quite often occurs in kangaroos and possums being hand-raised. The signs of this disease are grey-white blobs in the mouth and throat, and often a brown saliva which stains the lips, resulting in loss of appetite because the mouth is sore. It can also show externally with bald patches of skin that are bumpy and swollen, and pale coloured diarrhoea which gives the animal a foul yeasty odour. The treatment is oral drops of Nystatin or Mycostatin (prescribed by a veterinarian), for a 1500 g animal usually 0.5 ml three times a day for the first two days and then 0.5 ml twice a day for seven days after that.

Coccidiosis (*Eimeria cunnamullensis*) is quite common in Eastern Grey Kangaroo joeys. It is also prevalent in wild groups, where it usually affects young at foot joeys at the stressful stage after they are permanently kept from the pouch. It causes acute black diarrhoea containing blood, and death usually follows a rapid decline in the animal's condition. Very occasionally with very strenuous and dedicated care an animal can be saved.

The symptoms of salmonella infection are similar to those of coccidiosis and death can be rapid. Quick treatment with antibiotics and subcutaneous fluids can save lives. Salmonella often affects young animals, especially if they are kept in overcrowded conditions.

Brittle bones Just as it is with children, sunshine is important in the development of healthy bones in young macropods. Insufficient sunshine may lead to bones which are brittle and break easily. Thus it is important from the time they are furred that joeys get a sufficient amount of sunshine, daily if possible. This does not mean they must be put out to graze; it is sufficient to take them outside in their bag or basket when you are gardening, or hanging out the washing, making sure they do not get chilled or overheated.

Pneumonia If an animal's breathing is noisy or uneven, its temperature is unusually low or high and/or it is lethargic, have it checked by a veterinarian immediately. It could have a respiratory infection or have ingested milk into its nasal passages or lungs. A non-mobile joey being treated for pneumonia should be turned regularly from one side to the other at least every two hours and gently massaged.

Intestinal worms and parasites Many native animals are subject to infestations of various intestinal worms, capillaria worms and the parasite toxoplasmosis, as discussed on page 92.

Ectoparasites (see page 92)

Working out a joey's age

One of the first things to determine is an orphan's age. From this you can judge whether or not it is possible to safely and reliably raise it. Table 4.1 on page 30, which dates the appearance of various physical features in the pouch life of several species, may help you make this assessment.

Tables 7.1 to 7.8 below give growth measurements for a number of species of different sizes, which should give you a basic idea of your orphan's approximate age. Take foot, tail, leg and head measurements of the joey following the diagram.

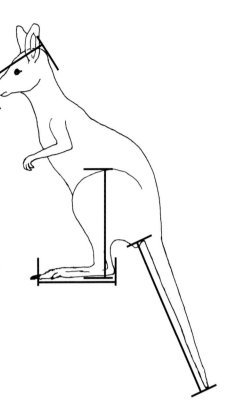

The measurements most commonly used in ageing macropods are the foot, leg, head and tail measurements, in association with weight. The head measurement is taken from the nose to the back of the skull, the foot from the back of the heel to the end of the toe (excluding the claw), the leg from the top of the knee to level with the bottom of the foot (with the foot held at right angles to the leg) and the tail from the rump to the tip

Table 7.1 Growth measurements of Tasmanian and Rufous Bettongs

Age in days		30	40	50	60	70	80	90	100	110
Tasmanian Bettong	Foot (mm)	29	42	53	63	71	79	85	93	102
	Weight (g)	25	50	60	70	130	140	150	200	280
Rufous Bettong	Foot (mm)	16	20	25	30	42	53	73	85	110
	Tail (mm)	30	40	52	65	80	100	125	160	220

Note: Figures for Tasmanian Bettong adapted from R. J. Taylor et al (1987); figures for Rufous Bettong adapted from P. M. Johnson (1978)

Table 7.2 Growth measurements of rock-wallabies and potoroos

Age in days		40	60	80	100	120	140	160	180	200
Allied Rock-wallaby	Head (mm)	20	30	38	42	50	60	65	70	78
	Foot (mm)	15	25	30	40	50	70	85	93	107
Yellow-footed Rock-wallaby	Head (mm)	27	33	40	50	56	60	72	80	85
	Foot (mm)	18	28	40	52	68	90	110	125	–
Long-footed Potoroo	Head (mm)	27	36	45	55	68	81			
	Foot (mm)	17	27	41	56	73	90			
	Tail (mm)	31	50	85	120	182	248			
Long-nosed Potoroo	Head (mm)	22	31	42	50	60	68			
	Foot (mm)	11	18	26	45	55	66			
	Tail (mm)	25	43	80	115	148	181			

Note: Figures for Allied Rock-wallaby adapted from R. L. Close et al (1990); figures for Yellow-footed Rock-wallaby adapted from W. E. Poole et al (1985); figures for Long-footed Potoroo and Long-nosed Potoroo adapted from J. H. Seebeck (1992)

Table 7.3 Growth measurements of some small wallabies

	Age in days	60	80	100	120	140	160	180	200	210
Quokka	Foot (mm)	17	24	32	43	55	67	77	84	88
	Tail (mm)	35	49	65	88	115	145	175	199	203
	Weight (g)	21	39	67	106	167	240	430	670	835
Tasmanian Pademelon	Foot (mm)	25	35	45	55	70	80	90	100	105
	Tail (mm)	35	55	75	90	115	135	165	195	215
	Weight (g)	65	100	150	210	280	425	680	950	1100
Parma Wallaby	Foot (mm)	21	29	38	51	65	82	97	104	107
	Tail (mm)	45	65	80	105	136	181	240	280	290
	Weight (g)	23	43	66	103	146	248	429	620	752
Agile Wallaby	Foot (mm)	25	40	55	65	115	144	150	164	170
	Tail (mm)	50	85	116	150	205	260	320	390	420
	Weight (g)	35	84	165	315	555	865	1315	1820	2100

Note: Figures for Quokka adapted from J. W. Shield (1961); figures for Tasmanian Pademelon adapted from W. R. Rose et al (1982); figures for Parma Wallaby adapted from G. Maynes (1972); figures for Agile Wallaby adapted from T. H. Kirkpatrick et al (1969)

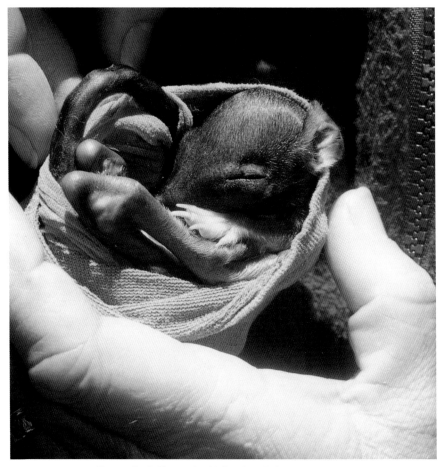

Two-and-a-half month old Brush-tailed Bettong joey

Five-and-a-half month old Red Kangaroo joey

Tammar and Black-striped Wallaby joeys, both nine-and-a-half months

Northern Nailtail Wallaby, five months old (Ian Morris)

Table 7.4 Growth measurements of some larger wallabies and kangaroos

	Age in days	140	160	180	200	220	230	240	250	260	280
Whiptail Wallaby	Foot (mm)	60	70	110	150	170	175	180	185	190	–
	Tail (mm)	160	210	260	320	390	425	450	480	510	–
	Weight (g)	245	435	580	785	1150	1375	1580	1815	2035	–
Red-necked Wallaby	Foot (mm)	54	57	62	67	97	126	148	158	165	175
	Tail (mm)	150	180	220	260	320	350	380	400	420	440
	Weight (g)	540	710	895	1100	1370	1560	1815	2110	2305	2700
Red Kangaroo	Foot (mm)	115	150	170	200	220	230	232	235	240	
	Tail (mm)	185	230	290	350	415	440	470	495	520	
	Head (mm)	75	85	90	100	112	120	122	128		
	Weight (g)	620	890	1220	1620	2820	3610	4400	5200		
Euro	Foot (mm)	95	120	143	166	174	182	187	191		
	Tail (mm)	180	225	275	332	357	385	402	420		
	Weight (g)	385	550	800	1400	2400	2900	3400	–		
Wallaroo	Foot (mm)	110	140	160	180	190	195	200	205	210	220
	Tail (mm)	200	250	300	360	420	445	470	485	500	540

Note: Figures for Whiptail Wallaby and Wallaroo adapted from T. H. Kirkpatrick (1985); figures for Red-necked Wallaby adapted from T. H. Kirkpatrick (1985); figures for Red Kangaroo adapted from H. J. Frith et al (1969); figures for Euro adapted from E. H. M. Ealey (1967)

Table 7.5 Growth measurements of Eastern Grey Kangaroos

Age in days	140	160	180	200	220	240	260	280	300	320
Foot (mm)	70	100	140	170	180	200	210	220	230	235
Tail (mm)	160	200	230	260	300	360	430	480	510	540
Weight (g)	735	975	1250	1600	1885	2260	2790	4020	5135	6155

Note: figures adapted from W. E. Poole et al (1982)

Table 7.6 Growth measurements of Western Grey Kangaroos

Age in days	120	150	180	210	240	270	300	330	360
Head (mm)	62	74	85	96	105	113	120	129	135
Hind foot (mm)	59	80	103	127	150	174	195	203	210
Tail (mm)	120	164	212	263	315	367	416	453	487
Weight (g)	213	410	735	1245	2010	3015	4585	6175	7910

Note: Figures adapted from W. E. Poole et al (1982)

Table 7.7 Growth measurements of Tammar or Kangaroo Island Wallaby

Age in days	160	180	200	220	240	260	280	300	320	350
Head (mm)	54	60	65	70	74	78	80	82	84	86
Hind foot (mm)	74	85	107	115	125	130	133	136	138	140
Leg (mm)	85	102	121	140	152	158	166	170	173	178

Note: Figures adapted from C. H. Murphy et al (1970)

Table 7.8 Growth measurements of Swamp Wallaby

Age in days	140	160	180	200	220	240	260	280	300
Head (mm)	64	72	80	84	87	91	96	99	103
Leg (mm)	90	113	136	149	164	175	185	195	204
Foot (mm)	75	90	115	126	135	142	148	153	157
Weight (g)	300	450	650	960	1350	1825	2400	3250	3750

Note: Figures from J. C. Merchant, personal communication, CSIRO data (1998)

Assessing age by tooth eruption

Incisor tooth eruption appears to happen about the time that the pouch young starts releasing the teat, e.g. in the Red-necked Pademelon (pouch life 180 days) the first pair of incisors come through between 120–130 days of age, the second pair at around 150 days and the third pair soon after the joey is permanently out of the pouch. In the Long-nosed Potoroo (pouch life 105 days in the wild, 125 days in captivity) the lower incisors erupt at around 60 days and are fully through by 70 days, which coincides with the teat release stage. Premolars start erupting just after 70 days of age and take about 20 days to fully erupt; molars start showing shortly afterwards.

‣ 8 ‣

Heating and Housing

First days in care

We have found that the best way to get a newly orphaned joey to accept a substitute (human) mother, especially if it is hairless or just growing short fur, is to put it in a flannelette bag down inside one's T-shirt. The combination of body warmth and movement feels more like the mother's pouch. We feel it is important that macropod young should have plenty of company in the early stages of raising. At this time the young in the wild is constantly with the mother in her pouch. The joeys, especially older ones, can also be nursed in their pouches to aid in the bonding process, which is further strengthened by grooming. Using this method we feel that the joey accepts the voice and body scent of its substitute parent more quickly. Smell is an instinctive tool of recognition in natural situations. Anything that makes the first stressful days of settling in easier is very important to the animal's well-being.

Noise

Until the new orphan has settled into its new surroundings, excessive noise (like hammering, vacuuming, loud music and party noises) should be avoided close to the animal. The animal should be kept well away, securely, in a quiet room. However, if you keep them too protected from everyday sounds they can become over-nervous when they are old enough to be outside and experience noisy cars, planes, screeching birds, and so on. This is a hard line to judge, as the animal needs to remain nervous of noises associated with humans, cars and dogs if it is to survive after release.

Pets

It is essential not to allow orphan joeys to be housed near pet cats or dogs. These animals are predators. When the joey is released into the wild it must retain its instinctive fear of all predators to enable it to escape from potential attack.

Orphaned wildlife are not domestic pets. They cannot be trained like cats or dogs, so do not expect them to react in the same way to commands. Do not allow children to play with them, or take them to school for 'show and tell'.

Thermoregulation

During the first half of its pouch life a joey cannot maintain its own body temperature and is reliant on the mother's pouch to regulate its warmth and humidity. During this stage the pouch entrance is kept fairly tightly closed, only being opened when the mother puts her head in to groom the joey or lick its urogenital opening to encourage urination or defecation. Marsupial young start to thermoregulate (keep themselves warm for short periods out of the pouch) just after halfway through their pouch life. By the time they are permanently out they can totally regulate their own temperature (unless they are ill).

Maintaining body temperature

Heating methods include (human) body warmth, sheepskins, heat pads, hot water bottles, electric blankets, heated room.

Hairless wallaby joeys and joeys whose skins are just colouring with the fur under the skin can be placed in a little pouch and carried next to the carer's skin during the day and put in their artificial pouches at night. One of the problems with artificial heating is that very young joeys tend to dehydrate easily; with body warmth they do not seem to dehydrate as readily, especially at first when they may not be drinking enough milk. If the skin appears dry, gently rub in a thin layer of warmed pure olive oil, baby oil or Sorbolene cream once or twice a day. Once the fur grows in, the problem will go away. Sometimes when the new fur is growing they have flaky dry bits of skin like dandruff, but there is no need to worry about this. The larger hairless young (kangaroos) do not seem to dehydrate as easily as the smaller species but they can also be oiled when necessary.

In winter very short furred joeys can be accommodated in a pouch made from full-fleece sheepskin or artificial sheepskin, with a sheepskin lid to keep the winter chill out. This is used in conjunction with an inner flannelette bag that the joey sits in, and an outer woollen bag around the sheepskin, the whole lot placed in a basket or thick canvas haversack. Healthy joeys maintain their own body temperature sufficiently this way. If the animal is not staying warm enough one of the other heating alternatives should be used as well. A hot water bottle must be monitored regularly to ensure that it is still providing warmth—if the water temperature drops too low the joey will become cold and stressed.

The best way to check the temperature is with a

A nine-and-a-half month old Swamp Wallaby standing by her hanging pouch. Swampies are browsers so she enjoyed chewing the she-oak branchlets near the pouch

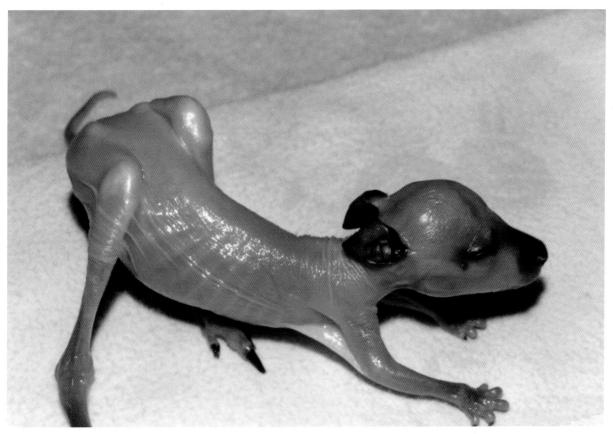

This little four month old Swamp Wallaby has been lightly oiled to prevent its skin drying out. This joey's eyes are very close to opening, as the eyelids are quite well developed (Dennis Browning)

thermometer. Around 32–34°C (90–94°F) is ideal. Checking the temperature with your hand is not always a good guide— if your hand is cold the joey will appear warmer, and if your hand is very warm the joey may feel cool.

The most satisfactory inner bags are made of cotton flannelette with rounded corners, and the fluffier the flannelette the better. If the joey urinates in the bag the moisture passes through the fabric and the animal remains dry. If you have a joey that continually urinates in the bag, despite being toileted regularly, cut up old cloth nappies or towels into oblong pieces that can be wrapped around the animal. When the joey makes a mess or wets the towel, it will often kick the towel out of the way and thus doesn't get so wet or dirty.

Fleecy-lined cotton tracksuit tops and woollen jumpers, with the sleeves cut off and sewn across and the neck opening sewn up, make good outer pouch bags.

Hanging pouches

A hanging bag with a stiffened opening is a good idea for joeys which have reached the stage of jumping in and out of their pouches on their own. The stiffened edge allows the joey to find the opening and roll in easily, as it does in a mother's pouch. An inner lining of cotton or flannelette can be pinned in place with baby's safety nappy pins so it can be changed easily. The pouch should touch the floor, resting on a thick mat or folded towel so that the joey can jump in and out safely without hitting its head when entering the bag, and be insulated from the cold floor. The pouch should be large enough to enable the joey to lie on its side; this helps them get used to the feeling of lying on the ground out of the pouch. These pouches can also be used outside as a refuge until the joey feels secure enough to hide under a bush. If the

joey is kept in a large basket, pin one side of the pouch or pillowcase to the handle to allow the joey to get in and out easily. Jam one side of the basket under a chair or cupboard so that it does not topple over.

Pet pads which are regulated to a constant temperature are useful, but they can get too warm. Control the heat by putting layers of towels or blankets between the pad and the joey until the correct temperature is reached.

Electric blankets can also be used but remember that you cannot fold them or bend them as they can form hot spots and catch fire; it is also very important that they not be urinated on, so protect them with a plastic sheet covered by another blanket. Electric blankets with multiple heat settings can be adjusted quite easily to the correct temperature.

A light globe (preferably 15 watts) fixed inside a large box will heat the interior to about 30°C (90°F). Make sure that the animal cannot touch the hot globe and that the globe will not burn any part of the box as well. The light must not shine in the animal's eyes.

The best way of utilising the heat from a light globe is in conjunction with a wooden box with a false floor made from pegboard (or plywood with several holes drilled through it). Mount a light globe under the false floor, with a dimmer switch on the outside, to regulate the temperature. This is much safer than having the globe inside the box with the joey. The joeys can be laid flat on a blanket in their pouches or hung in bags from the sides of the box.

The ideal temperature-controlled surrounding for joeys, or any orphaned animal, is a thermostatically-controlled heated room in which the orphans do not have to be heated individually, where if they do uncover themselves or get out of their pouches they will still be warm, especially in the winter months.

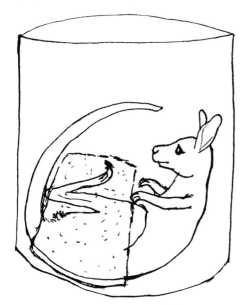

How to position the cloth nappy around the joey in a round-cornered pouch

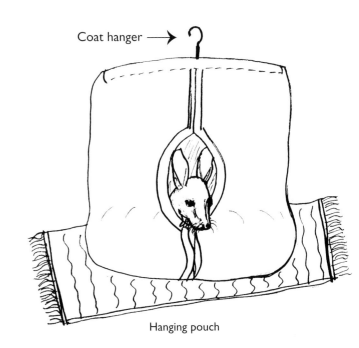

Hanging pouch

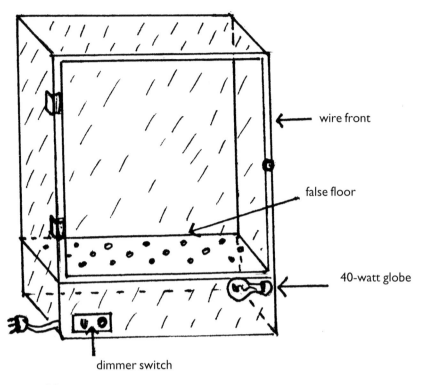

The wooden nursery box designed by Dennis and Yvonne Browning to keep their joeys in a constant temperature environment. The box is 60 cm wide x 65 cm high x 45 cm deep

wire front

false floor

40-watt globe

dimmer switch

Temperature problems

Getting cold It is because of the uncertainty of artificial heat that we try to avoid using it if possible. Every time that a joey is put back in its pouch, especially if the weather is changeable, the temperature must be checked to ensure the animal will neither overheat nor get too cold. Never allow a bag or basket to be in a draught.

Healthy furred joeys should be able to maintain their own temperature if they are snugly bagged. At night make sure that inner bags are securely tied, with plenty of leg room for stretching. You don't want them getting out and getting cold and lost in the middle of the night.

We have found that keeping joeys too warm on artificial heat tends to retard their fur growth, so that the first coat is very thin and patchy. Once they are moving about in and out of the pouch the coat thickens and becomes normal in a few weeks.

Sometimes you come across a young joey (short-furred) that will insist on getting out of its bag in cold weather. If you do not wish to tie it in the bag during the day, cut armholes in a sleeve cut from a woollen jumper and slip this over the joey to give it some protection against the cold. Don't leave it on all the time though—they can get tangled in it and they need to be able to groom themselves.

Overheating If joeys kept in the house are becoming active out of their pouches in winter, fireguards around fireplaces and heaters are essential. Because of the insulation properties of their fur, joeys do not seem to sense heat at dangerous

levels and run the risk of becoming singed, even burnt. It is safer to install heaters on the wall out of reach.

Rock-wallabies and other cool forest-dwelling species do not cope well with temperatures over the low 30°s C (90°F). It is important to keep an eye on maximum temperatures, especially when such joeys are at the permanently out of the pouch stage. Rock-wallabies in the wild live in rocky areas where they can move about and select caves or crevices which can be up to 15°C (20–30°F) cooler than the outside temperature, while the forest-dwellers

Joey in a sleeve

move into cool damp gullies when surrounding temperatures become too high. Watch the temperature during heatwaves.

Exercising pouch young

Unfurred joeys should be massaged or gently moved about in their pouches after each feed to exercise their muscles. This mimics conditions in the mother's pouch, where a joey is subject to constant movement as the mother moves about. Short-furred joeys can be put out for a few minutes in a warm environment to exercise their muscles and lungs, important for their well-being. Older joeys should be allowed to get in and out of their pouches when they wish.

A seven-month-old Red Kangaroo peers about from her comfortable sheepskin-lined basket. The back edge of the basket is jammed under the chair to prevent it tipping over

·9·

How to Feed

Many Australian fostercarers have devised their own formulas and methods which work very successfully. If your animals are healthy, strong and grow correctly then stick with what you're doing. However, it is essential to remember that kangaroo joeys cannot digest lactose and may develop cataracts if fed on cow's milk; they will inevitably develop diarrhoea on straight cow's milk (Tanya Stephens 1975). The specially prepared milk formulas Digestelact, Di-Vetelact, Wombaroo and/or Biolac are essential items on a carer's list of supplies. See Appendix B (page 101) for information on suppliers.

Emergency formulas

In an emergency you can feed a joey with glucose and warm water (1 teaspoon glucose to 100 ml water), using either a small bottle and teat available from veterinarians and pet shops, an eyedropper, or a bike valve on the end of a syringe. (An older joey may lap efficiently out of a small dish while you hold the animal securely wrapped on your lap.)

Before Digestelact came on the market we made up our own formula, which was 125 ml Carnation Evaporated Milk (not sweetened) diluted 50/50 with boiled water, to which we added an egg yolk and 3 drops (not droppers) of Pentavite vitamin supplement, plus ¼ teaspoon calcium carbonate powder to each 250 ml of milk mixture. This can still be used in an emergency if other milks are unavailable.

Prepared milk formulas

Biolac is a successful formula especially researched and designed to suit joeys' digestive systems.

Wombaroo milk formula has been very intensively

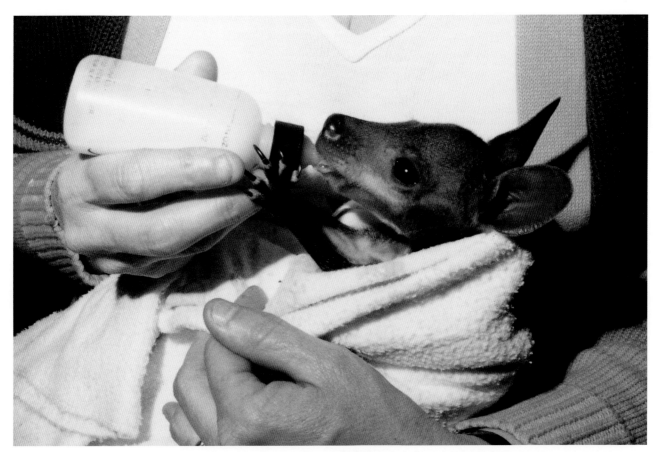

A Swamp Wallaby enjoying her milk. Once joeys are in the routine of feeding they need not have their head held or eyes covered unless they are easily distracted by what is going on around them when they are supposed to be drinking (Dennis Browning)

researched and developed to be as close to a kangaroo's natural milk as possible. The milk powder, feeding details and growth charts are available from the suppliers listed in Appendix B and from veterinary surgeries. Note that the feeding charts supplied with Wombaroo are only relevant to Wombaroo milk formulas.

Digestelact milk powder is a low-lactose human baby formula that can be obtained through your local chemist.

Digestelact is made up following the instructions on the tin PLUS 1 egg yolk (sieved through a tea strainer so the 'skin' does not clog up the fine hole in the teat) per 300 ml. The addition of acidophilus yoghurt to the milk could aid in the development of gut flora, but this is usually only necessary for joeys whose gut flora balance has been upset by treatment with antibiotics or when there has been some other problem upsetting their digestive system.

When yoghurt is called for, add 1 level teaspoon of plain yoghurt to 100 ml of milk, mixing it in just before each feed. Continue this addition for three or four days, even though there should be a marked improvement in the formation of the faeces within 24 hours. We also find that the yoghurt stimulates the appetite.

Di-Vetelact milk formula, available from veterinarians, is basically the same as Digestelact.

Feeding equipment

Special teats and bottles, specially designed in different sizes for various sized kangaroos and wallabies, are available from Helen's Fauna Nursing Service, together with Wombaroo Milk and Feeding charts (see Appendix B).

Specially designed long thin teats, bottles and Biolac Milk Formula are available from Geoff and Christine Smith (see Appendix B). By the time a large kangaroo joey finishes drinking from its mother the teat it suckles from may be 5 cm long, so specialised teats are important.

Preparing and cleaning teats and bottles

Make a small hole in the teat by piercing the end with a flame-heated fine needle. It takes a little trial and error to get the right-sized hole. Start with a small hole rather than a large one if you have an enthusiastic feeder, because if the milk is delivered too quickly it can end up in the animal's lungs, causing pneumonia. If the animal is put off by the unaccustomed firmness of the teat (compared to its mother's teat), you may have to start with a large hole and change teats in a couple of days to one with a smaller hole once the animal starts sucking harder and the milk flow becomes faster. Too fast a flow results in milk spilling out of the sides of the joey's mouth or getting up its nose—if this happens the joey may jerk and cough during the feed or sound snuffly afterward. In either case hold the joey by the tail and pat its back until the milk is sneezed or coughed out. The correct flow results in a steady flow of small bubbles rising up through the milk in the bottle (just like feeding a baby). The milk flow can be slowed down by bending the teat at right angles to the joey's mouth, as shown in the illustration. A hairclip or paper clip can be put across the wide section to flatten the teat to slow the flow of milk as well. If an animal always drinks too fast from the teat and chokes on it, you may have to teach it to lap from a dish. This often works quite well with wallabies, but not with the larger kangaroos.

Cleanliness is essential. Thoroughly wash and rinse out teats and bottles immediately after each feed. Only lukewarm water should be run through the teats; using hot water will enlarge the hole and harden the teat. Use a sterilising liquid like Milton's obtainable from chemists and supermarkets.

Preparing formula

Fresh milk formula should be made up every 24–36 hours, and kept refrigerated until required. Only the milk required for each feed should be heated, and any leftovers from a feed must be discarded, to avoid contamination. If you only need small amounts of milk for a little joey, to avoid fiddling about you can make up a larger amount and freeze it.

How much do I feed?

A joey being fed Digestelact, Di-Vetelact or Carnation Milk formula should drink about 10–20 per cent of its body weight each day, e.g. a 500 g joey should be consuming 50–100 ml in a day; if you are using Biolac the ratio is 10–15 per cent of body weight daily (50–75 ml formula for a 500 g joey).

When using Wombaroo milk formulas you must adhere strictly to the instructions given with the product.

Frequency of feeding

Hairless joeys Very young hairless joeys will have to be fed every two hours during the day and, depending on how much they take at each feed, through the night every three hours until they are taking their full daily rations. If the animal seems healthy, is drinking its daily milk requirements and looks as though it will cope without the 3 am feed then drop that feed—feed at midnight and then again at 6 am.

Furred joeys Furred joeys, if they are drinking sufficiently at four-hourly feeds during the day, can be left at least seven or eight hours overnight, especially if they are starting to nibble solid food. Some of this can be put in or near their cloth pouches when they are put to bed at night. Small amounts of grass, tender short pieces with a few little roots and soil attached are preferred. Joeys seem to like nibbling on soil when first eating solids—it has been suggested that this helps to establish gut flora. A piece of dry bread or dry biscuit (e.g. Sao or Salada) can be given as an alternative. Fresh bread is a no-no, as it sticks to the roof of the mouth and can cause the joey to choke.

Feeding technique

For the first couple of days a joey is in care its milk should be made up at two-thirds strength; you can switch to full strength after that. To feed the joey its warmed milk, hold the animal's head, gently covering the eyes with your thumb and index finger either side of its muzzle. Position it snugly in a warm pouch, either sitting up or lying sideways. Don't lay the head back, so that if too much milk does enter its mouth the excess will spill from its lips rather than going down into its lungs. Never squeeze the bottle or otherwise force milk into a joey's mouth, as they can easily choke. At first you may have to encourage the joey to take the teat into its mouth—do this by putting your hand around the animal's head and gently inserting your index finger into its mouth on one side and sliding the teat partway in, then taking your finger out so its mouth closes on the teat. Keep your hand over the animal's head, covering its eyes, so that the head is kept still. After a few days this may not be necessary as some orphans are only interested in drinking their milk. Some animals will start to suck straight away and others will just spit the teat out. In such a case try dripping just a few drops of milk onto the joey's lips so that it gets the taste of it. They usually cooperate when they become hungry. If a joey is particularly stubborn, retire from the fray and try again in a couple of hours—you will probably have more success.

It will often take a few days for a joey to adapt to the feeding regime and take the required amount at each feed, as they have to abandon the habit of sucking continually from their mother's teat, taking only a small amount at a time. Initially you may have to be patient, and sit for up to half an hour until the joey has taken enough. You have to encourage them to take a full feed allowance in one go, or you will be sitting feeding all day, and a carer has a life to lead too! After each feed clean any spilt milk from around the joey's mouth and body and stimulate it immediately to go to the toilet.

A good gauge as to whether an animal is taking enough milk in the first day or so is whether the yellow droppings from the artificial milk come through the animal's system 24 to 36 hours after the first feed. The natural droppings of a young animal that is not yet eating solids are a dark green/brown colour in a toothpaste consistency. An older animal should have solid pebble droppings.

After a week or two on artificial formula the joey's system should have settled and its droppings should be a yellowy/green colour in a toothpaste or plasticine consistency. Once you have them settled on a formula, try to avoid changing it.

If a joey reacts to the milk formula with diarrhoea then stop feeding the milk for 24 hours and (if the animal will drink it) feed a glucose and warm water mixture (5 ml glucose to 100 ml water); then slowly start again with a 25 per cent strength milk formula, increasing it daily by 20 per cent until you reach full strength. If the joey still has problems a change in formula or a veterinary check of its faeces may be necessary. It can sometimes take a couple of weeks for a joey's stomach to adapt completely to the artificial milk formula.

Weaning

When the joey is spending large amounts of time out of the pouch and is eating solid food it should be weaned onto lapping milk out of an unspillable dish on the floor. Some joeys, especially wallabies, will take to the dish easily. Some wallabies will drink from a dish when they are quite small, but you must nurse them on your lap at this stage. The larger species often take longer to transfer over to a dish. Sometimes one has to go to the extreme of letting a joey suck the milk out of the dish through a teat, until eventually the teat is lowered into the milk and the joey gets the hang of having the milk around its lips while lapping. Occasionally, if a joey is being particularly stubborn, sprinkling a little Milo on top of the milk will speed up the changeover.

At the permanently out of the pouch stage I delete the egg yolk from the formula and cut the number of feeds down to three a day if the joey is eating solid foods (grass and/or cubes), then gradually down to twice a day, then once a day, until their natural weaning time. This can be worked out for most species from the table on page 31. Most macropods appear to drink from their mothers, after they are permanently out of the pouch, for about half the length of time they spend in the pouch, e.g. Red Kangaroos, with eight months pouch life, drink until they are twelve months old, and Pademelons (six months pouch life) drink till about nine months old. Grey Kangaroos have an exceptionally long weaning period—after 10–11 months in the pouch they drink till 18 months of age.

To help slow down the flow of milk through the teat, the bottle and teat may be held at right angles, thus flattening the teat, or a hair grip or paper clip can be put across the wide part

Toileting

Orphan joeys need to be stimulated to urinate and defecate. Use a tissue or warm, damp cotton-ball to stimulate them by gently stroking the cloaca (external opening), and catch the results in a small 'potty' container. (Use this to fertilise your indoor or outdoor plants after mixing it with water.) Cleanse the container thoroughly after each use. The best way to position the joey when you are using the pottying method is to lay it on its side in the pouch and hold the small container under its cloaca while you stimulate it.

Some hand-raised joeys old enough to venture outside the pouch will want to get out of the pouch to urinate, this being the natural procedure in the wild. The female kangaroo will lick the urogenital opening to stimulate the joey to urinate when she ejects it from the pouch for exercise. They will often pee automatically on soil or grass when put outside to exercise. Stimulating hand-raised joeys after every feed works very well—even very young hairless joeys soon get used to this routine and hold on to their urine and faeces between feeds, which helps to keep the pouches (and the joeys) clean and warm.

Wet or dirty pouches should be changed as soon as possible, remembering to warm the clean liner for very young joeys, especially hairless ones, in cold weather.

For the joeys (often male) that cannot hold on all night, we recommend feeding and stimulating them to urinate about an hour before you go to bed, and stimulating them again just before you put them to bed. If this does not work, put a baby's disposable nappy in the bottom of the pouch to stop the animal getting wet, or put a blue-striped nappy liner under the joey; this also helps to keep the joey drier as the fluid passes through it. Nappy liners only work for quite young hairless or just furred joeys, because the older ones wriggle about too much. If a joey does wet itself and become cold, it sometimes seem to get a chill and for the next couple of days will wet itself more often. Fortunately they seem to settle back into the routine of holding on again.

Joeys that can stand well can be trained to go to the toilet on a towel or a flat tray of cat litter (covered over by fine openweave material to prevent the animal eating the litter). Stand the animal on the towel and stimulate it to urinate. After this has been done a few times the animal will be able to smell its own scent in this area and with luck will continue to use the towel or tray; some species seem to learn quicker than others. If the joey's food can be put in the same area, the toilet is more likely to be used regularly. Make sure that the towel or litter is changed often and that the food is placed in untippable plastic or pottery bowls.

Unfortunately, when a joey has the run of the house favourite places to hop onto and urinate always seem to include lounge chairs and the middle of the bed! This becomes a bad habit and is very hard to break.

Solid food

When joeys are old enough to spend quite a lot of time out of their pouches solid food—pelleted food, lucerne hay, fruit and vegetables (chopped apple, carrots, sweet potato)—can be provided. Lucerne hay is better than lucerne chaff for young animals as it does not have as many sharp-cut ends that may injure their mouths. The pelleted food can be kangaroo cubes (see Appendix B), or chicken/guinea pig/rabbit pellets. Large cubes should be crushed into smaller pieces. A bowl of fresh water should always be available.

Regurgitation Macropods will regurgitate some food back into their mouths for re-chewing, especially after they have eaten something too quickly. It looks fairly dramatic when you first witness the contortions and coughing sounds which accompany this action, but it is a natural occurrence from the time they begin eating solid foods.

Indoor facilities

On slippery floor surfaces (polished wood, lino, slate), it is advisable to have heavy non-slip carpet mats in areas where the animals could slip over when they are hopping about, especially where they change direction. This is especially important for the larger species which tend to be less sure-footed/more clumsy than the wallabies.

Keep indoor potplants out of reach, especially if you do not know whether they are poisonous or not. Certain species, like Swamp Wallabies, wallaroos and rock-wallabies, are very agile and will hop onto the backs of lounge chairs and then onto tables, cupboards and shelves if given the opportunity—never underestimate their jumping abilities.

The Older Joey

Outside facilities

A growing joey requires a secure, enclosed yard that is both dog-proof and child-proof. Solid wood or steel fences are preferable. The ideal situation is to have purpose-built holding yards adjacent to forested areas suitable for the release of species known to occur in the region. In reality, many carers live in urban areas and are restricted to garden environments. This is one of the reasons that halfway housing facilities for the period between hand-rearing and final release are necessary.

There are many things to think about in providing an outside environment. For many of the wallaby, pademelon and rat-kangaroo types it is beneficial to have non-poisonous bushes and shrubs, native if possible (see Appendix A) in the garden for them to play amongst, to shelter from the heat, to sleep under during the day or just to use as a hideaway if they feel threatened. It is natural for many young wallabies in the

Female Eastern Grey Kangaroo having a play tussle with her young at foot

wild to sit under bushes waiting for their mothers to return from feeding areas which may be a few hundred metres or even a kilometre or more away. Wallabies usually sit on their tails in shallow depressions dug under these bushes, with their backs against tree trunks or fences.

A handy shelter for rat-kangaroo joeys is a little igloo made from fibreglass or cement, which must be large enough for them to take grass or hay into for making nests. These should be positioned in cool areas under shrubs or trees. Another simple shelter for wallabies can be made from small light-gauge bird-mesh netting and fencing wire. Just double a panel of wire mesh over a layer of green, leafy branches, ferns or canvas. Weave the fencing wire along the top, bottom and centre, making sure you leave at least 15 cm sticking out either end to anchor the shelter to the ground. If you put the shelter against a fence or wall under a bush, it won't need a back; if you want it free-standing under a shrub the structure can be bent to make its own back wall. Make sure that there are no sharp bits of wire sticking out.

Shelter sheds should be positioned in shady areas away from the perimeter fences, especially if the sheds are low enough to help the wallaby jump out over the fence. Pellets, lucerne hay and/or fruit and vegetables can be placed in these shelters in large containers which keep the food off the ground. A small room (old unused laundry, etc.) attached to the house could also be set up as a secure refuge. A constant water supply, in an unspillable dish out of the sun, should be available at all times.

As bettongs and potoroos can climb quite well, perimeter fences made of wire-netting must have a large inward-facing overhang. Solid wooden or corrugated iron fences should be fine, as long as you ensure that efficient diggers, which many small macropods are, can't dig their way out.

Probably not too many people have the chance to raise rock-wallabies. These are lively little characters, very agile, who can leap from shiny bookcase surfaces to other surfaces very easily, even when quite young. They instinctively jump up on objects, so provide their yards with a secure pile of wooden boxes to jump about on and hide in. Hang heavy cloths in front of some of the boxes to imitate the caves they like to hide away in during the hottest parts of the day in their natural environment. Such constructions must be at least three metres from the perimeter fences. Rock-wallabies are also quite capable of jumping up sloping tree trunks and branches, so eliminate such temptations from the edges of the yard.

Red Kangaroo joeys in particular like to scratch hip-holes in the soil, as do Greys and Wallaroos, so do not be surprised if you end up with bare patches of soil in many areas of the yard. Reds often lie on their backs in these hip-holes, sunning themselves. For these larger species the perimeter fence should be at least two metres high.

Weeds

The garden or enclosure to be used to house joeys should be checked for any known poisonous plants and these should be removed. Regular checks are necessary for poisonous annual weeds such as petty spurge (*Euphorbia peplus*). The symptoms of *Euphorbia* poisoning are: coughing as though there is something stuck in the throat, contorting and twisting with an upset stomach, lethargy. They may froth at the mouth, and refuse to eat or drink. Sometimes the legs appear stiff and awkward. We find it is best to put the affected animal in a very loose pouch, lying on its side so it has plenty of room to stretch; if the animal wants to get up and move about, however, let it—to force it to stay in the bag will probably stress it further. Symptoms generally ease within 4–10 hours of the plant being eaten, when the animal should begin eating and drinking again as normal. Twenty-four hours later they will have a little diarrhoea, but that only lasts for about an hour.

As a general rule watch out for and remove all plants that have a milky sap. See Appendix A, page 101.

Handy hints

'Joey-sitting'—do not speak or let them smell you If you are asked to joey-sit another carer's pouch orphan, when you come to feed it do not speak or let it smell you before you put the bottle of milk to its mouth. This way, because the joey uses voice and body scent as recognition factors, it will still think that its foster mother is the one handling it, and be less likely to become upset. Once they are drinking they are less likely to get upset than when you are trying to get them to take the bottle. Let them smell you after they have fed, when they are more content.

Passing a joey on to another carer If you know that an orphaned joey will have to be passed on to another carer in a few weeks (if possible, immediate transfer is preferable) allow it to get used to a variety of handlers early on. Once the joey has settled in, after a fortnight or so, let someone else give it a feed (under supervision) at least once or twice a day, so that it becomes used to being handled by more than one person— in this way the transfer to the new carer will be less traumatic. Pass the animal over with some of the pouches that it has been using; these familiar articles will help the joey settle.

Some joeys which are hand-reared on their own can become quite obsessive about having contact with only one person; it is suggested that such animals be handled by other people, under supervision of course, prior to being moved. An animal which has been raised on its own does not usually take long to integrate with its own kind, providing it is done as a gradual process to minimise stress.

Getting an animal used to being outside When you are getting an animal used to staying outside by itself, it pays to be a little sneaky. Often the animal will follow you to the gate, or panic when it sees you leaving. We find that if you wait until it becomes sleepy in the warm sunshine, or disappears behind a bush, you can sneak out quietly. This appears to be less stressful for the animal than watching you leave or shutting the gate in its face. Those foster carers with children will understand these tactics—a bit like leaving clingy children at school.

Natural behaviours

Among the many species of macropods, the gregarious types that live in groups, like Grey and Red Kangaroos, are usually calm and mix easily with humans, while those which live solitary lives tend to remain highly strung or shy in captivity, hiding when visitors come. This is not consistent for all individuals, of course, but is true in general. Individuals can be calm and relaxed in one wildlife park, where humans are in constant contact with them, but moved to a new park or enclosure may react quite differently and become quite wild and unsettled. Some of the wallabies, like Agiles and Whiptails, tend to be highly strung, especially the Whiptails; even young joeys can become stressed and die in a matter of a few hours despite being cared for properly.

Many behavioural studies done on captive groups and free-ranging wild groups of macropods have found that their behavioural habits, sexually and socially, are very much the same. Most of a kangaroo's habits appear to be instinctive and very few, if any, have to be taught by their mothers. Most of the animals that we have hand-raised have mated effectively and produced and raised young successfully when assimilated into captive groups, or have been released successfully to survive many years in the wild.

The many instinctive traits that joeys practise without having a kangaroo mother to teach them include basking in the sunshine, selecting certain types of grass, nose-sniffing and quivering when meeting new animals or people, breeding and grooming themselves as soon as their fur begins to grow. With some, it's digging hip-holes, or knowing where to hide—wallaroos hide behind shelters or under bushes, just as in the wild they utilise caves, crevices and shrubs in rocky habitats. Even when parrots or other birds give alarm signals they seem to react automatically, becoming alert and looking about for the danger.

If you have the pleasure of sitting and watching family groups of macropods in the wild or even in large enclosures or parks you can observe many of their behavioural habits. It can be very helpful for fostercarers to do this as it helps you to understand some of the actions of your orphan joeys. Many of the natural reactions seen in normal family groups show up instinctively when they are hand-raised; for example, the shaking they exhibit when someone strange comes up to them is how they react to each other until they get close enough to sniff and identify the other.

Play-fighting is something all joeys like to do, especially the young males who are preparing themselves for competition with other males when they are older and vying for dominance in their groups for the privilege of mating with the females. In wild groups you often see young ones play-fighting with their mothers or other members of the mob about the same age.

A young which strays too far from the mother and tries to get in the wrong female's pouch (or even a male's stomach) will be gently cuffed on the head. The mother usually calls her young with a clucking sound to which the young often responds as it returns. We often use a clucking call for joeys in care, and find they respond (naturally) faster to this than to calling them by name. If a joey becomes lost, the mother moves about looking and calling for it until it is found—the joey will also call to her with a loud coughing sound. It has been observed that Red, Eastern and Western Grey Kangaroo, Common Wallaroo and Antilopine Wallaroo females isolate themselves from the rest of the group while their young are almost at the young at foot stage, possibly so that the joey does not get confused and run to the wrong mother or so that a female joey does not get hassled by males (Jarman & Southwell 1986).

Some wallaby species use communal feeding areas in the wild, especially where grazing areas are adjacent to forests populated by several species, but go off on their own to their sleeping areas. Rock-wallabies appear to live in groups, but this may be an illusion due to the limited size of their specific rocky habitats.

Wallaby joeys tend to be more independent than the young of the larger kangaroos, which remain at the mother's side at the young at foot stage. Wallaby and pademelon joeys are often left sitting under shrubs while their mothers are out grazing. Rock-wallabies, as soon as they are permanently out of the pouch, are left in a rocky crevice at night; the mother comes back for the joey to suckle.

When the mother grooms the young in the pouch she sometimes gently forces it out for a run, licking it to stimulate the joey to urinate on the ground at the same time. Joeys sometimes appear to go berserk at this time, letting off steam by kicking their feet sideways, rushing away from the mother in all directions and back again. Some appear to get frustrated if they are not allowed back in the pouch immediately and do this crazy rushing about. Some hand-reared joeys exhibit similar behaviour—a Swamp Wallaby female that we raised would nip our legs when thirsty and dash about madly in frustration if her milk didn't appear quickly enough.

·11·

The Rehabilitated Joey

The ultimate goal of hand-raising an orphaned macropod is to release it back into its original habitat or into a captive group. Hand-raised wallabies, because of their more independent natures, adjust more readily to changes of surroundings and homes than the larger species.

Releasing into a captive group

Releasing a hand-raised joey into a captive group is a little easier than preparing it for release into the wild. Initially it is suggested that the joey be taken to a halfway house as often as possible while it is growing up, so that it recognises the area when it is ready to move there. When the time comes to get the animal used to the area, for the first couple of weeks it needs to spend a few hours each day, with the carer initially, in the yard it is to be put in—preferably with another quiet animal or joey that it has been raised with or with the group that it may have come from originally. When the animal appears quite calm and moves about comfortably in this new area, it should be taken there during the day and left there, perhaps with a familiar rug or bag in the shelter shed as a 'security blanket'. This process is repeated daily for the next couple of weeks. A special treat that they do not get at home—a Salada biscuit, fruit—can be given to them to associate with the new area. This process of acclimatisation is always less stressful if you have a pair of joeys that can keep each other company.

Eventually the joey is left overnight when it looks as though it has settled in (some actually start to object to going back in their bag to go home). If this happens to be in the middle of a cold spell (either summer or winter, as Australia's weather is so changeable) a heater could be set up on the wall of the shelter shed to help keep the joeys warm at night for a couple of weeks until they are completely settled in.

Ultimately, when they are totally at ease with the halfway house routine they can be put in with their own species (if they are not already), usually without any problems.

This process is flexible, depending on the nature of the joey and weather conditions.

Releasing into the wild

The feeling of satisfaction that comes with releasing a hand-raised animal into the wild is hard to beat. To return to a release area months later and find that the animal you spent so much time and effort raising and preparing for release has survived for that time and established itself is even more satisfying.

There are many ways of readying an animal for release. The ideal situation is to be living in the area of final release. At the University of New South Wales Field Station at Fowlers Gap, north of Broken Hill, hand-reared Red Kangaroos and Euros from the area were held in enclosures until they were weaned. At this point their yards were left open to allow them to wander freely around the homestead until they eventually assimilated with the wild groups of their own accord.

The same regime can be applied to solitary species, which can be relocated as a group to an enclosure for a few weeks. Once they get used to the area and appear settled the barrier can be taken away to allow the animals to come and go as they please until they feel confident enough to go off on their own. To help them over the assimilation period the supply of pelleted food or hay should be maintained until it is obvious that the animals are not relying on it.

This form of release should only be used where a carer can be on hand to watch for dogs and foxes worrying the animals or getting into the enclosure.

If neither of these options is possible the animals may have to be released directly into a National Park, forestry land or conservation park, preferably not in a picnic or camping area where they will have contact with humans. Contact the appropriate authorities to arrange such a release. Depending on the temperament of the various species or individuals, a dose of Valium is advised to slow them down and encourage calm investigation of their new surroundings.

The area of release for any species must have the appropriate habitat, an ample supply of natural food, and be within the natural distribution range of the species. It would not be wise to perform a release in times of drought or flood. Releasing animals into the wild is better done with a group which has been kept together for some time so that they have each other's company (until they decide to go off on their own if they are solitary types). If possible check them from a distance for a few days for their reaction to their new surroundings and to see that they appear healthy.

·12·
Management and Housing of Captive Groups

Kangaroos and large wallabies

Enclosures To keep large macropods in captivity on a permanent basis you need to have twice as much space for enclosures as you would be using at any one time, so that the animals may be moved from one yard to another to rest the soil and allow grass and other vegetation to regenerate. Ideally you should allow at least 125 square metres per adult kangaroo—more if you have the space. An enclosure 30 m × 25 m is reasonably adequate to house seven Grey Kangaroos, with a relief yard of equal size. Rotation of yards also lessens the density of faeces on the ground, which correspondingly lowers risk of disease.

Larger numbers of smaller species, such as the Parma Wallabies and pademelons, could be kept in an area this size.

Natural earth is the ideal ground surface, although animals can be held in concrete yards for a time; these must be raked and hosed and kept very clean. Concrete can cause problems, however—the animals' feet and tails can be damaged by constant abrasion from a rough surface; conversely, if the surface is too smooth, the animals are in danger of slipping over and harming themselves when it gets wet.

Fencing The ideal enclosure is circular, as there are no corners for animals to trap themselves in if they become frightened; in reality circular yards are impractical in terms of maximum ground usage. Square enclosures should be built with round steel posts or star-pickets on the outside of chainlink mesh or wire netting so that when animals run around the yard they cannot get caught between post and netting. Extra wire netting can be put across the corners to make more of an inner curve to the fence. Where there are adjoining enclosures

A wooden-fronted shed with doorway and an access door at the side for the carer. Wire guards are placed around the trees to prevent the animals chewing them. Branches and logs can be given to the animals to supplement their diet

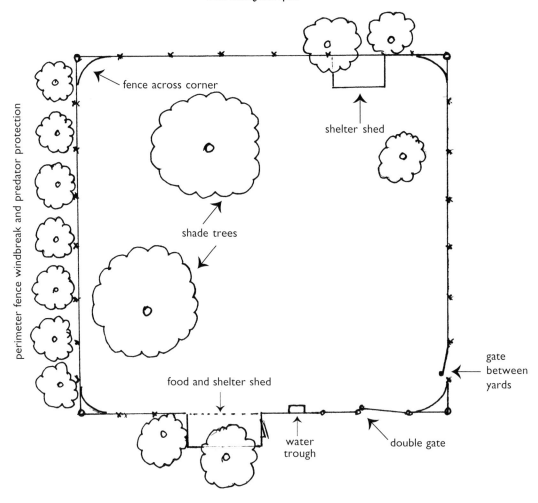

An ideal yard for keeping macropods

wire netting should enclose the posts that will be on the inside of the next yard.

Perimeter fencing around yards holding captive animals should be at least 2 metres tall and preferably of a solid material to stop feral dogs and foxes harassing the animals by running up and down the fences. If wire netting must be used for perimeter fencing, it must be chainlink mesh, and either dug into the ground directly below the fence for 30 cm or a skirt of wire at least 30 cm wide each side of the fence buried under the surface.

The preferred netting for internal fences is galvanised, 1.05 m wide, 4 cm hole size, made of 1.4 mm wire. Plastic coated wire is more expensive but the animals can see it more easily and tend to have fewer collisions with the fence. A larger mesh like pig-wire is not safe because if the animals run into it broken limbs and neck injuries may result from getting stuck in the large holes.

Internal fences need to be at least 1.8 metres high; three rows of straining wire are sufficient to support two widths of netting between posts 5 m apart—one strand along the top, one through the centre supporting the join between the two panels of netting and one at the base. Corner posts should be of 10 cm round galvanised steel pipe with angle supports. Again, bury a 30 cm strip of netting at the base of the fence to prevent animals escaping underneath it.

Build fence lines away from large-trunked trees to lessen the risk of a frightened animal colliding with the trees.

Gates Install inter-connecting gates near the front of the yards so animals may be moved easily. Gates can be left open overnight for a few nights until the animals are used to them being open and either move into the next yard themselves or can be gently encouraged to go through. The main gate to each yard should be large enough to allow entry of a small truck or tractor.

Shelter sheds Two open-fronted shelter sheds should be provided for each yard—one facing north, the other facing south, to give the animals a choice during inclement weather. Sheds can be made of corrugated iron covered in half logs to keep them cooler in summer and warmer in winter, or be made entirely of wood. Shadecloth stretched over wire netting and suspended a few centimetres above the roof helps reduce rain and hail noise on corrugated iron roofs. Install keeper-access doors on the side or back of each shed so that animals do not feel threatened by keepers coming in from the front. Warn animals of your arrival by making loud footsteps or calling out.

Where animals are kept in climates colder or hotter than their natural environment, fill in the front of the shelter shed leaving a 1 m opening at one end, or fill in the top half of the front. Extra warmth can be provided by a heater, out of reach on the wall. A heater for extra warmth will be necessary for sick or injured animals, or young animals which have to be housed outside during cold winter months. These sheds also provide a dry area for the provision of food.

Water troughs Continuously self-filling aluminium water troughs, fitted with ball-valves, should be positioned near the front of the yards for convenience of cleaning and to lessen disturbances. Taps which have to be placed inside the yards should be kept away from the fences to prevent agitated animals colliding with them when they run around. Taps can be attached to large white painted posts to make them more obvious, or situated in a covered pit in the ground.

Vegetation Where a perimeter fence is made of wire netting or link mesh, it is advisable to plant fast growing, thick low native shrubs close together outside the fence to provide a windbreak as well as a visual deterrent to predators. Established large shade trees in the yards and shrubby trees over the shelter sheds provide the ideal set-up for hot summers. Medium-sized shrubby trees hanging over the sheds lessen the risk of large heavy branches falling on the roofs. Shrubby trees also reduce the noise of rain and hail on corrugated iron.

Smaller wallabies and pademelons appreciate the extra natural cover provided by small shrubs and grass bushes planted in clumps along the inside of an internal fence or solid perimeter fence. Protective tree guards should be used to prevent the animals ring-barking live trees. Logs and leafy branches, particularly from stringybarks and other rough-barked trees, can be put in the yards as sources of extra roughage.

Kikuyu is a good sturdy grass which can be bought as turf rolls to lay in the yards—unfortunately not a particularly cheap exercise. It is a summer grass so a winter grass needs to be mixed in with it to provide winter fodder. Kikuyu is a durable grass and if rested regularly will survive very well with watering during dry spells. It is, however, classed as a noxious weed in some areas and may need to be controlled to prevent it spreading from the enclosures. The disadvantage of grassed enclosures is that more maintenance is involved with weeding, fertilising and watering. Higher numbers of animals can be kept in dirt yards, the disadvantage here being problems with soil erosion and a high faecal count which can result in disease.

As each State has many different types of vegetation, depending on climate and soil types, consult your local plant nursery for advice on the most suitable fast-growing, sturdy and long-living plants for your enclosures.

Regular checks for poisonous plants and weeds are essential.

Food Lucerne chaff and kangaroo cubes (see Appendix B) or chicken pellets can be supplied ad lib in metal hoppers in the shelter sheds. Lucerne hay can be provided in a hay rack with a lid so that it cannot be pulled out over the ground and walked on, but this system has the disadvantage that the stalks are wasted and must be cleaned away regularly. On the other hand, lucerne chaff can have sharp pieces that may pierce the animals' gums, possibly causing lumpy jaw. There is usually very little wastage if good quality chaff is used. If grass is available in the enclosure, feeding lucerne is usually not necessary.

Pellet bins 1 m long × 20 cm high × 30 cm deep with a top that slopes to the back of the bin, leaving an opening of about 25 cm, discourage young macropods from getting in the bins and defecating and urinating on the food. A bin 1 metre long allows a few animals to feed at the same time. A dish of chopped apples, carrots and sweet potato is appreciated as an occasional supplement to the diet.

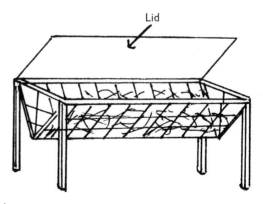

Pellet bin and hay rack

Hand-feeding small quantities of stale bread two or three times a week helps calm and tame the animals, enabling the catching of an individual by the tail, so that its pouch or general condition can be examined. Less stress is caused to the rest of the group in the yard if an animal does not have to be chased to be caught.

Hospital cages Hospital cages are essential for holding sick animals that need a clean area to recover from an illness or for new animals that need a secure area to adjust to new surroundings. When dealing with a diseased animal it is easier to control the infection if the animal can be isolated in an area that can be effectively disinfected.

Hospital cages are best built with concrete floors that are slightly roughened. Indoor cages should have good drainage so that they can be disinfected and hosed thoroughly. Outdoor cages should also have slightly sloped floors so that cleaning water runs into a drain outside each enclosure and into a grease trap that can contain disinfectant if required.

Ideally a hospital cage has an outdoor and indoor section. The indoor part should measure a minimum 2 m × 2 m square and be equipped with a light and heater well out of reach of the largest kangaroo. A dividing door between the two sections is necessary so the animal can be locked in or out during cleaning or kept locked in for warmth.

The outdoor section can be about 2 m × 4 m with a concrete floor, linkmesh sides and roof so that any animal can be kept in safety—large enough to allow an animal to move about easily, but not large enough to allow it to get up sufficient speed to hurt itself. If very nervous or 'wild-captive' animals have to be hospitalised, put up hessian or shadecloth around the sides of the cage to discourage them from damaging themselves by trying to get through the wire. Install a self-filling water trough at the front of the cage, which can be cleaned easily without having to enter the cage.

These cages are often handy to accustom hand-raised joeys to a new area—they are safely enclosed, but they can still hear and see the surrounding environment. It is good to have a larger yard attached to these hospital cages as well, so that sick animals can be rehabilitated separately from their own group until they have totally recovered.

The light fittings and heater in this hospital enclosure are well out of reach. Hessian has been put up around the sides to prevent restless animals attempting to get through the wire

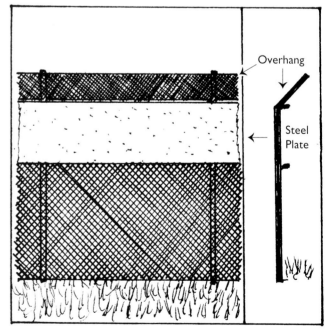

Fence showing wire overhang and/or steel plating

Quokka resting under a grass bush

Rock-wallabies and tree-kangaroos

Enclosures With these agile animals care must be taken that there are no sloping trees or branches within 3 metres of the perimeter fences or walls. Rock-wallabies often like to sit in the branches of trees, especially thickly vegetated trees providing a cool refuge. Rock-piles made from large boulders with caves, nooks and crannies to hide in are beneficial to rock-wallabies for shade and shelter, as they do not like rain or heat. For tree-kangaroos provide an above-ground feeding tray and a tree-house for shelter, even though in their natural habitat they feed on the ground as well as on tree foliage.

Perimeter walls for rock-wallaby and tree-kangaroo enclosures should be of solid smooth materials, like steel sheeting, concrete or brick, so that the animals cannot climb out. If a wire netting perimeter fence is used, fix an inward-facing overhang of netting at the top of the fence with 75 cm wide solid steel plating fixed along the top of the fence.

Food Nutritional requirements for tree-kangaroos, because they are folivores, are met by providing as many greens as possible. If you live in an area where appropriate rainforest trees are available, feed them naturally, otherwise provide a substitute diet of vegetables such as spinach, lettuce, Chinese cabbage, sweet potato vine (*Ipomaea batatas*), fig leaves, fern leaves, carrot tops, artichokes, oat grass, tree lucerne (*Cytisus proliferus*), sweet potato, corn, cucumbers and green

bananas (they eat skin and all). Other fruit and vegetables can be provided, as well as standard kangaroo pellets and dry dog food. Bread can be hand-fed to each animal so a dominant or greedy animal is prevented from hogging it all.

Rock-wallabies eat the same foods as kangaroos and large wallabies (page 87).

Bettongs and potoroos

Enclosures Enclosure requirements for bettongs and potoroos are similar to those for rock-wallabies, but if you are likely to have predators like pythons, snakes, foxes or cats come calling, it is advisable to house them in fully roofed enclosures. Use 1–2 cm wire linkmesh, with fibreglass corrugated sheeting to protect the feeding area—about one-quarter of the roof. The wire mesh should be dug into the soil at least 40 cm to prevent the animals digging their way out. As potoroos, which are not as strictly nocturnal as the other rat-kangaroos, like to sun themselves, provide an area where they can get access to the sun in the early morning or late evening. Shade can be provided by growing native vines over part of the cage.

Vegetation Another important requirement for bettongs and potoroos is plenty of cover to hide in. Tussock bushes (*Poa australis*) are an ideal yard planting for the animals to build their nests in or make their squats under; they do not usually need boxes or shelters if this kind of vegetation is available. They seem to prefer making their own homes. Supply a large pile of straw, hay or long stranded dry grass which they will carry to their nesting sites using their semi-prehensile tails. Large hollow logs and wooden nest boxes can be provided as alternatives to tussock grasses.

Food Potoroos and bettongs do well on dry dog food, kangaroo cubes, a variety of root vegetables such as sweet potato, potato, parsnips and carrots, and fruit such as apples, oranges, bananas, pawpaw or other seasonal fruit available. Feeding must be carefully monitored in these animals as they can easily become overweight. A bettong, for example, only requires half an apple, pear and banana, one medium carrot, half a slice of bread and a quarter of a cup each of dog kibble and kangaroo cubes daily. This diet is also suitable for potoroos, in slightly smaller amounts. Animals kept in outside enclosures will catch and dig up their own insects; if the soil is regularly watered more of this natural food will be encouraged to move into the area.

A successful diet for Musky Rat-kangaroos incorporates rolled oats, unsalted raw peanuts, cracked corn, oranges, apples, sweet potato, dog chow, chook pellets, grasshoppers and earthworms. Once again, if the animals are kept outdoors in natural soil yards they can supplement their own insectivorous part of their diet.

Ratio of males to females in captivity

Even though Pademelons, Parma Wallabies, Tammar Wallabies and Bettongs are solitary species, they can be kept in groups like the larger animals. However, one must be careful to monitor the number of males in an enclosure. Dominant males will often fight inferior males to the death. If a less dominant male is being unduly picked on, it is best to move it to a separate enclosure. Females can also be over-harassed by too-numerous males when in oestrous and can become very stressed, being unable to escape from their advances. A few males can usually be kept peacefully together if there is no female around.

Introducing a new animal

When introducing new animals into a yard, hessian or shade cloth should be hung on all fences to prevent them colliding with the wire netting, which they can find difficult to see if they are running wildly. Sometimes the smallest noise will set off a panic.

Catching a Red Kangaroo joey with a handnet

A condition known as capture myopathy can occur in macropods not sedated with Valium to calm them. The symptoms are increased respiratory and heart rates leading to muscle stiffness; if the animal is still hopping about, the head tends to hang down and flop about. Electrolytes, vitamin E supplements and Diazepam should be prescribed. Keeping the animal quiet in a hospital cage for a few days, with or without the above treatment depending on the severity of the condition, can also aid the animal's recovery. Unfortunately, the end result is often death.

Catching

If a large joey, wallaby or kangaroo has to be caught the preferred method is to grab its tail close to the rump and pass your other arm under its forearms across the front of the ribs—be careful though, some will bite.

Small wallabies and young at foot can be caught with a bag net made from a hessian sack sewn to a padded metal hoop attached to a long wooden handle. Catch the animals quickly as they run along the fence line, and transfer them to hessian bags hung on the fence to prevent them rolling about.

A third method, appropriate for kangaroos and the larger wallabies, involves using a 10 m long double wall of 8 cm mesh shark netting with a 2.5 metre drop. A rope is threaded along the top edge of the net and tied to a fence so that it is held secure when an animal gets caught. The net is laid on the ground and when the required animal runs towards it the net is pulled up just in front of it. The timing has to be just right, as the animal will turn away if the net comes up too soon. This method requires at least three and preferably five people to make it work correctly. You need a couple of people to chase the animal towards the net, another ready to catch it as soon as it is caught in the net, and others ready with a wool pack or bag to bag the animal as quickly as possible.

A common reason for catching animals in an enclosure is to mark them in some way for identification. Various techniques of identification are explained in Appendix E (page 105).

Bagging

When placing a macropod in a bag (holding the bag away from any solid obstacles) make sure that its head curves forwards as though it were rolling into a pouch. A macropod neck is reasonably fragile and can easily become damaged. Remember to hold their kicking hindfeet away from your body (or other people) as they can cause serious injuries. To stop a wallaby thrashing about while you are putting it into a bag, twist the whole animal gently while holding it above the ground by the tail. Make sure the animals are in the pouch position in the bags and then hang them up. Larger species can be put into wool packs.

Transportation

Animals being transported in bags should be suspended to prevent them hitting anything if they are thrashing about. Quiet animals probably do not need to be sedated, unless it is a very long trip, in which case Valium as prescribed by a veterinarian can be used to calm them. Vehicles used for transport should be well ventilated, and travelling time should be early morning or late evening, or night-time when it is cooler, especially in summer.

If the trip is going to be longer than three or four hours, transport the animals in custom-built crates or wooden boxes. As they tend to push upwards to escape, the tops of the boxes should be made of wire netting padded with bags stuffed with straw or foam rubber to help prevent head injuries. The animals should be tranquillised (enough to slow them down and still maintain their thermoregulation, but not enough to put them to sleep). The crates must be large enough for them to stand up and lie down comfortably, but not large enough for the tail to stretch out behind them. Food should be provided for trips longer than about 10 hours and water should be given whenever the vehicle stops, for a break or overnight, especially during hot weather.

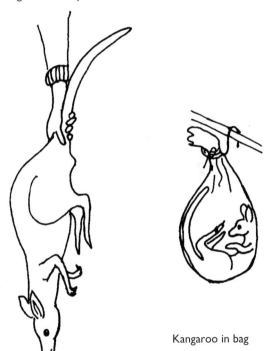

Kangaroo held by the tail

Kangaroo in bag

·13·

Common Illnesses

Always seek veterinary advice before treating any animal. It is best to get diseases verified before treating them with any medicines. New treatments are being discovered all the time. A veterinarian should be consulted for dosage rates of any treatments or sedatives before they are administered.

The diseases most commonly encountered in macropods in captivity are toxoplasmosis, gastrointestinal coccidiosis, intestinal worms, lumpy jaw and capillaria worm infestations.

Coccidiosis (*Eimeria cunnamullensis*) See also page 66. This disease can become rampant in captive colonies of Grey Kangaroos if the animals are kept in small enclosures where the infective oocysts (eggs) can survive in very damp grassy areas. It often multiplies after long periods of wet weather when the Greys are more susceptible, especially the younger animals. For this reason alone, having extra enclosures is essential so that animals can be moved from an infected yard after they have been treated. An anti-coccidial powder such as Amprolium (which some manufacturers include in kangaroo food cubes) can be mixed with their food pellets every two months to act as a deterrent, especially if there are new animals or young permanently emerging from the pouch, in case of persistent wet weather or if the faeces show a high oocyst count.

Necrobacilliosis or **lumpy jaw**, a disease that can affect most macropods, results in gross bone distortion, particularly in the jaws. It is most common in captive colonies but does occur in the wild. The symptoms are lesions in the mouth and swelling of the jaw, lips, tongue or head; a bad mouth odour is also present. The infection can be caused by a bad tooth, eating sharp pieces of food or a head injury. Animals always fed on soft foods develop a soft lining to the mouth and become more susceptible to mouth injuries. Treatment often involves surgery to remove infected teeth and bone, combined with Oxytetracycline injections, but the infection usually recurs. Eventually the animals end up in poor condition because they have difficulty eating and have to be euthanased. Infections can also occur in the foot and tail.

Intestinal worms A variety of tapeworms and roundworms have been recorded in macropods, both in the wild and in captivity. *Strongyloides* can occur in large numbers, particularly if an animal is stressed. Macropods usually carry a certain number of these worms naturally, but if an overgrowth occurs the animal develops diarrhoea, loses condition and becomes very lethargic. A faecal sample should be taken immediately to a veterinarian if an animal scours for more than a day or two, especially if the motions are particularly smelly. There are several worming products available to treat animals orally and also powders that can be regularly put on their pelleted food to act as a preventative measure. Pastes such as Telmin can be put in a sandwich and hand-fed to tame animals once every three months or when the faeces, which should be checked regularly, show a high worm count. Telmin also comes in granules that can be crushed and added to the food (see Appendix B for suppliers). Panacur is another worming treatment that can be given orally.

Capillaria worms have been detected in bettongs and potoroos; if untreated they may cause fatal respiratory failure. Colonies found to be infected by this threadworm need to be wormed with an Ivomec subcutaneous injection every three months (see Appendix B for suppliers).

Toxoplasmosis (*Toxoplasma gondii*) is a protozoal parasite that has two life stages—one infects only cats while the other can be present in cats and other animals. Various symptoms occur when this parasite invades an animal—most often no symptoms are noticed, sometimes a mild illness occurs, or in some cases severe illness and death. When animals survive an initial infection they form tissue cysts and antibodies to fight any future infections.

Australian wildlife has not evolved with cats and therefore they are susceptible to this disease. Macropods can pick up oocysts while grazing if they eat grass that has been in contact with kittens or any cat faeces containing the parasite's oocysts.

The most common route of infection is eating lucerne hay from a barn where kittens have been living. Kittens are usually infested with the parasite when they eat their first mouse, or meal of raw meat; the oocysts are subsequently deposited on the ground with their faeces. Thereafter the kittens are immune to future infection; adult cats are not usually a source of infection unless they missed out as kittens.

Ectoparasites Kangaroos are not normally infested with fleas but pick them up if housed in areas harbouring dog fleas. A cat flea-powder (cats are sensitive to many of the same chemicals as macropods) can be used to rid a joey of fleas, but make sure you do not leave excessive powder on the fur.

As kangaroos groom their fur with their lower incisor teeth and lick their grooming claws clean they risk ingesting some of the powder.

In tick areas, **bush ticks** and **paralysis ticks** attach themselves to macropods, often around the eyes, in the armpits and along the inner thighs, places where the skin is very soft. Sick animals seem to gather excessive ticks, possibly because they are not grooming efficiently. A few ticks generally do not bother a healthy animal, but the eyelids can become irritated and swollen if numerous ticks are present there. Most macropods living within paralysis tick zones acquire an immunity to the tick's effects after only a couple of weeks.

Only if they get too heavy an infestation initially will they become ill, becoming uncoordinated and eventually totally paralysed, usually resulting in death. Animals from a tick-free zone introduced into a tick-infested area are likely to be more susceptible to tick paralysis.

The **wallaby fly** (louse fly) of the family Hippoboscidae is another insect found on kangaroos and wallabies. They are brown, greatly modified blood-sucking, flat-bodied, robust-legged flies. The 12 mm adults live as ectoparasites in the fur of their hosts. They do not get to plague proportions and do not appear to bother the animals, except when they are biting.

·14·
Behavioural Notes

Observation of surroundings

Joeys from a very young age, some even before they are furred, poke their heads out of their mother's pouch (or their fostercarer's snug-bag) and look around at their surroundings. By the time they get to following their mothers about they know their home range quite well. Reflecting behaviour in the wild, hand-raised joeys will treat rearrangements of their environment with great suspicion, creeping very slowly up to any new item or looking warily about.

Macropods in general have a set pattern of movements daily to and from feeding and resting areas; probably by the time the young is permanently out of the pouch they know most of the routes used.

Red Kangaroo joey looking about from the safety of its mother's pouch, clearly showing the distinctive nose pattern (George Filander)

Instinctive reactions

Kangaroos are generally afraid of dogs that are larger than cats, although they will often chase small dogs and cats. Never let a joey get used to dogs, because it might not regard them as enemies when it should.

Animals are generally said to be afraid of fire, but possibly are more afraid of the noise associated with bushfire than of the flames themselves.

Snakes do not automatically cause terror. On a videotape recording the night-time movements of a group of Tammar Wallabies a large python was observed moving through the yard. The animals were seen to move towards the snake, sniffing it from a short distance and jumping back, and then going forwards again—they appeared much more curious than scared.

Escape behaviour

Various field trips and adventures into outback areas have given us the opportunity to observe the way different species react to human approach or disturbance. When a group of Red Kangaroos is disturbed they will often scatter in all directions; the young at foot do not necessarily follow their mothers and vice versa, even though they are gregarious. When a group of Grey Kangaroos is disturbed they usually hop off as a group; if one or two animals get ahead of the rest they will often stop and wait until the main group catches up. It is safer to be in a group, as solitary animals are more susceptible to predators.

This behaviour seems to be instinctive in these species of kangaroos because joeys that we have raised have shown these same traits. Red joeys tended to run and run in a new environment, whereas Greys ran a certain distance and waited for the others to catch up. If there was more than one following, the joey would wait for the whole group to catch up before going on.

Rock-wallabies tend to zip away secretly into a crevice or boulder heap and sit quietly until danger has passed; if you get too close to one in a cave or crevice it will race straight past you to escape.

Reactions to handling of pouch young

Many kangaroos will not hold their pouches tight or will eject a pouch young after they have been handled by keepers.

These Western Grey Kangaroos were quite relaxed once they had checked out the friendly photographer and went down to drink peacefully before casually hopping off

After handling, some Tammar Wallaby females have been observed to attack fully-furred pouch young, biting and kicking them to prevent them getting back in the pouch. To return smaller or hairless pouch young that have been dropped from the pouch, the female must be caught and the young put back in the pouch (if it was taken off the teat, the teat must be put back into the joey's mouth). The entrance to the pouch is taped shut with masking tape so that the young will not fall out. Within a day or two the tape will come off or be pulled off by the female, by which time the pouch young has lost the human smell and the female has calmed down. This method usually works and the female keeps the pouch tightly closed.

Curiosity

A fascinating experience that I have enjoyed many times is sitting by a small dam, tank or waterhole in warm weather in the outback and waiting for the wildlife to come and drink when the temperature is dropping and the sun has almost set. If you sit close to some shrubbery so that your outline blends in with the surrounding habitat, you can wait for kangaroos, birds and other wildlife to arrive. From our experience, especially if the wildlife in the area has not been chased or hunted, as long as you are sitting quietly before the kangaroos arrive they tend to accept you as part of the surroundings. As long as you sit reasonably quietly you can even change camera lenses and gently slide about changing position—the animals just look at you and then carry on with what they were doing. The pair of Western Grey Kangaroos in the photo appeared from behind a bush about four metres away; out of curiosity they came to within two metres of me, had a close look and a sniff and sauntered down to the water to have a drink.

One of my most interesting experiences one evening during summer was while I was staying at Fowlers Gap, north of Broken Hill. I sat next to a water tank that was visited regularly by the local Euros. Within a short time there were twelve Euros of various ages three to fifteen metres away from me. I even opened up the camera bag to change lenses because they came too close for the 200/500 zoom. It is a really exciting experience to sit amongst wild kangaroos and watch them acting naturally without being afraid of you.

Even while tracking animals in the wild you may be able to get surprisingly close, as happened with a pair of Agile Wallabies. I was standing right out in the open in a sandy creek bed within a few metres of them when they turned around and looked at me. I stood very still and they did not appear to recognise my silhouette as an enemy outline. They react totally differently to dingo or eagle outlines. Presumably these animals were not regularly pursued by humans; otherwise they would have been more wary.

Ignoring intruders

Another interesting time to watch macropods is when they are busy fighting or mating—they tend to ignore their surroundings while involved in these activities. One night we walked right up to a pair of Rufous Bettongs involved in a mating ritual, getting close enough to touch them before they became alarmed and hopped off.

On two separate occasions in the bush we have come across Swamp Wallabies engaged in courting or mating rituals, and they have hopped right past and around us, within four or five metres, the males hardly giving us a sideways glance because they were so pre-occupied with keeping an eye on the female. On both occasions there were two males following one female.

Cross-breeding

An interesting occurrence of cross-breeding took place at a fellow carer's sanctuary a few years ago, where an Agile Wallaby female was kept with a group of Tammar Wallabies. One day she was discovered to have a newborn pouch young, having been mated by the male Tammar. This first young looked more like a Tammar and was male; the second young was female and had more Agile Wallaby features. The other curious feature was that Agiles have a six-month pouch life and Tammars between 8.5–9 months, but both of these young stayed in the pouch for only 7.5 months.

ENDNOTE

We hope you have enjoyed reading this book and have found it interesting and beneficial. We have learnt many interesting things ourselves while caring for our charges and have found the fostercaring experience very rewarding. Much of the behavioural information came from our own experiences and observations in our dealings with macropods, whilst watching their actions and reactions between individuals and family groups in captivity and in the wild.

We hope that you will now understand more of the different aspects of the macropod life cycle and the need to conserve these varied and fascinating creatures that inhabit our wilderness.

APPENDICES

Appendix A
Common poisonous plants and weeds

Angel's trumpet (*Datura* spp.)—flowers and seeds of all species

Azalea species

Blue-green algae on ponds and dams

Bracken Fern (*Pteridium esculentum*)—leaves

Cassia (*Senna coluteoides*)

Castor oil plant (*Ricinus communis*)—seeds; this plant is a declared noxious weed in some areas

Clovers—cause bloat

Coastal myall (*Acacia binervia*)

Cotoneaster (*Cotoneaster pannosus*)—berries

Crabapple (*Malus domestica*)—leaves and fruit

Crofton weed (*Ageratina adenophora*)

Deane's wattle (*Acacia deanei*)—leaves

Grass trees (*Xanthorrhea* spp.)

Hydrangea (*Hydrangea* spp.)

Holly (*Ilex aquifoliaceae*)

Jasmine—night-flowering species

Lantana (*Lantana camara*)—red-flowering type is more toxic

Liquidambar (*Liquidambar styraciflua*)—leaves

Lucerne—can cause bloat when fresh and green

Oleander (*Nerium oleander*)—wilted leaves

Privet (*Ligustrum sinense*)

Passionfruit (*Passiflora edulis*)—leaves

Peppercorn tree (*Schinus molle*)

Photinia (*Photinia glabra*)

Rhododendron (*Rhododendron* spp.)

Rhus (*Cotinus coggyria*)

Roses—some species

Rubber trees (*Ficus elastica*)—leaves

Solanaceae species—potatoes, capsicums, deadly nightshade, etc.

Soursob (*Oxalis pes-caprae*)

Sugar gum (*Eucalyptus cladocalyx*)—suckers and mature leaves, especially if wilted

Umbrella tree (*Schefflera actinophylla*)—new shoots

Wandering Jew (*Tradescantia albiflora*)

Wisteria (*Wisteria sinensis*)—new tendrils

Yesterday, today and tomorrow plant (*Brunfelsia australis*)—especially wilted leaves

White cedar (*Melia azedarach*)—berries especially

White moth plant (*Araujia hortorum*) climber—seeds

Appendix B
Hand-raising supplies and advice

Wombaroo Milk Formula

Wombaroo Milk formulas, teats, bottles and all information necessary for using this formula are available from:

New South Wales
Helen's Fauna Nursing Service (02) 4465 1328

Other states
Contact local veterinarians or Wombaroo Food Products, PO Box 151, Glen Osmond, South Australia 5064
Phone (08) 8277 7788

Kangaroo Cubes

Analysis: Crude protein, min 14.0 per cent, crude fat, min, 3.0 per cent; crude fibre, max 13.0 per cent; actual salt 0.75 per cent; fluorine, max 0.0096 per cent. Available in 40 kg bags from:

Young Stock Feeds Pty Ltd
133–135 Lovell Street, Young, NSW 2594
Phone (02) 6382 1666

Biolac Milk Formula

Biolac Milk, feeding instructions and teats; contact
Geoff and Christine Smith,
PO Box 93, Bonnyrigg, NSW 2177
Phone (02) 9823 9874

Worming solutions

Ivomec through Merck Sharpe and Dohme (Aust) Pty Ltd; available through veterinarians
Telmin granules and paste, through Smith Kline & French Laboratories; available through veterinarians

Appendix C
State fauna authorities

New South Wales
National Parks & Wildlife Service
43 Bridge Street (PO Box 1967)
Hurstville 2220
(02) 9585 6444

Australian Capital Territory
ACT Parks & Conservation Service
PO Box 119, Tuggeranong 2901
(02) 6246 2211

Victoria
Department of Conservation and Environment
123 Brown Street (PO Box 137)
Heidelberg 3084
(03) 9650 1195

South Australia
National Parks & Wildlife Branch
55 Grenfell Street, Adelaide 5000
(08) 8204 9000

Western Australia
Department of Conservation and Land Management
(CALM)
PO Box 51, Wanneroo 6065
(08) 9334 0333

Northern Territory
Conservation Commission of the Northern Territory
PO Box 496, Palmerston 5831
(08) 8989 4411

Queensland
Department of Environment and Heritage
160 Ann Street, Brisbane 4000
(07) 3202 0232

Tasmania
Department of Parks, Wildlife & Heritage
134 Macquarie Street (GPO Box 44A)
Hobart 7001
(03) 6233 6033

Launceston office:
PO Box 180, Kings Meadow 7249

Appendix D
Contact organisations for wildlife assistance

Australian Capital Territory

RSPCA (ACT) Inc.
Kirkpatrick Street, Weston Creek, Canberra.
PO Box 82, Weston 2611
(02) 6288 4433

Wildlife Foundation (ACT) Inc.
PO Box 207, Jamison Centre 2614
(02) 6296 3114

New South Wales

AWARE
(Australian Wildlife Ambulance Rescue Emergencies Inc.)
PO Box 592, Caringbah 2229
(02) 9525 0010

FAWNA (For Australian Wildlife Needing Aid)
PO Box 41, Beechworth 2446

Friends of the Koala
PO Box 5034, East Lismore 2477

Kangaroo Protection Co-op Trust Orphanage
51b Carters Road, Dural 2158
(02) 9651 2557

KPSN (Koala Preservation Society of NSW)
PO Box 236, Port Macquarie 2444

LAOKO (Looking After Our Kosciusko Orphans)
18 Kurrajong Street, Jindabyne 2627

NANA (Native Animal Network Assoc.)
PO Box 780, Ulladulla 2539

Native Animal Trust Fund (Hunter Region)
8 Conway Street, Toronto 2283
(02) 4967 4995

NTWC (Northern Tablelands Wildlife Carers)
PO Box 550, Armidale 2350

NRWC (Northern Rivers Wildlife Carers)
PO Box 6432, Lismore South 2480

RRANA (Rescue & Rehabilitation of Aust. Native Animals)
107 Boughtman Street, Broken Hill 2880

RSPCA NSW
201 Rookwood Road, Yagoona 2199
(02) 9709 5433

Sydney Metropolitan Wildlife Services
Lane Cove National Park, Lady Game Drive, Lane Cove 2066
(02) 9413 4300

Taronga Zoo
PO Box 20, Mosman 2088
(02) 9969 2777

TVWC (Tweed Valley Wildlife Carers)
PO Box 898, Murwillumbah 2484

WCGI (Wildlife Carers of Glen Innes)
PO Box 520, Glen Innes 2370

Wildcare Queanbeyan Inc.
PO Box 863, Queanbeyan 2620
(02) 6299 1966

Wildlife Animal Rescue and Care Soc. Inc.
PO Box 2383, Gosford 2250
(02) 4365 1121

WIRES (Wildlife Information & Rescue Service)
PO Box 260, Forestville 2087
(02) 9975 1633 or (02) 9975 1643

WIRES branches in:
Blue Mountains, Central Coast, Tamworth, Bathurst, Clarence Valley, Coffs Harbour, Far SE NSW, Wollongong, Narooma, Mudgee, Armidale, Snowy Mountains, Goulburn, Wagga Wagga, Bowral, Woolgoolga

Victoria

Department of Conservation & Environment
123 Brown Street, Heidelberg 3084
(03) 9450 8600
(Contact for 150 Regional Wildlife Shelters)

RSPCA Victoria
3 Burwood Hwy, Burwood East 3151
(03) 9808 5111

The Wildlife Care Network
PO Box 295, Mt Evelyn 3796
(03) 9457 6144

Tasmania
Department of Parks, Wildlife & Heritage
134 Macquarie Street, Hobart 7001
(03) 6233 6033

RSPCA (Tasmania) Inc.
PO Box 102, Launceston 7250

South Australia
Fauna Rescue
(Friends of Humbug Scrub Assoc. Inc.)
38 Allchurch Avenue, Redwood Park 5097

Marsupial Society of South Australia
GPO Box 2462, Adelaide 5001
(08) 8258 9999

National Parks & Wildlife Branch
General Enquiries Service
(08) 8204 9000

RSPCA (South Australia) Inc.
158 Currie Street, Adelaide 5001
(08) 8231 6931

Wildlife Welfare Organisation of South Aust. Inc.
27 Coronation Road, Strathalbyn 5255
(08) 8536 2071

Western Australia
Fauna Rehabilitation Foundation
The Brand Wildlife Centre
65 Camboon Road, Malaga 6062
(08) 9249 3434

FAWNA (Fostering & Assistance for Wildlife Needing Aid)
PO Box 551, Busselton 6280
(08) 9727 2170

Kojonup Wildlife Rescue
PO Box 133, Kojonup 6395
(08) 9833 6295

RSPCA (Western Australia) Inc.
7 Mallard Way (PO Box 463), Cannington 6107
(08) 9351 8377

Northern Territory
Conservation Commission of the Northern Territory
PO Box 496, Palmerston 5831
(08) 8989 4411

RSPCA (Northern Territory) Inc.
PO Box 40034, Casuarina 5792
(08) 8984 3795

Queensland
Inala Community Conservationist Association
71 Fernlea Avenue, Scarborough 4020
(07) 3203 5169

National Parks & Wildlife Service
PO Box 42, Kenmore 4069

Orphaned Native Animals Rear & Release (ONARR)

RSPCA (Queensland) Inc.
301 Fairfield Road, Fairfield 4103
PO Box 6177, Fairfield Gardens 4103
(07) 3848 0522

Appendix E
Tagging for research purposes

Marking or tagging is a good way of keeping a record of an animal's history. There are various ways animals can be marked for identification: collars, ear tags (metal or plastic), tattoos or ear-punched holes. For long distance identification, coloured round plastic sheep tags work well, if positioned correctly in the lower part of the ear so that the ear does not droop. These are most successful on kangaroos and large wallabies, but are less appropriate for small wallabies owing to the small size of their ears. Small numbered metal tags can be used on the smaller species; unfortunately they tend to get caught on obstacles and be ripped out of the ear, leaving quite a large tear. Tattooing is possible only on animals that have fairly naked, light coloured ears.

Collars are often used on animals being observed in behavioural studies. Collars for the larger breeds can be made from leather or conveyor belting riveted together around the animal's neck, making sure that it is not too tight and allowing enough room for growth if the animal is not an adult. One such collar survived for twenty-five years on a Red Kangaroo in a wild population. Different coloured reflective tape or numbers can be glued to the collars to help identify individuals. Nylon collars with adjustable buckles can be used on wallabies, with different coloured attachments for identification from a distance.

Ear punching is also used for identification. Using a sharp leather punch, with a piece of cardboard put against the back of the ear, a clean hole can be cut, making sure to avoid the many blood vessels that criss-cross the ear. If a blood vessel is accidentally cut, antibiotic powder and a cotton wool plug are applied as a healing measure. Ear punching appears to inconvenience the animals the least. The numbering method for this system works as ahown in the following.

Left Ear

1 – front ear, one hole
2 – tip ear, one hole
3 – back ear, one hole
4 – front ear, two holes
5 – tip ear, two holes
6 – back ear, two holes
7 – front ear, one hole + tip ear, one hole
8 – tip ear, one hole + back ear, one hole
9 – front ear, one hole + back ear, one hole
100 – centre ear, one hole

Right Ear

10 – front ear, one hole
11-19 – front ear, one hole + patterns for nos 1-9
20 – tip ear, one hole
21-29 – tip ear, one hole + patterns for nos 1-9

and so on . . .

LEFT EAR   RIGHT EAR

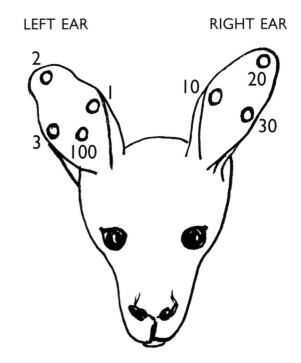

References and Further Reading

* These books available as reference books in bookshops and libraries.

* Aldenhoven J. & Carruthers, G. (film) *Kangaroos—Faces in the Mob.* Green Cape Wildlife Films.

* Archer, M. (1985) *The Kangaroo.* Weldon, Sydney.

Archer, M. and Clayton, G., eds. (1984) 'Vertebrate Zoogeography & Evolution in Australasia', in *Animals in Space & Time.* Hesperian Press, Perth.

* Archer, M., Hand, S. J. & Godthelp, H. (1991) *Riversleigh: The Story of Animals in Ancient Rainforests of Inland Australia.* Reed Books, Sydney.

Bailey, P. & Best, L. (1992) 'A Red Kangaroo, *Macropus rufus,* recovered 25 years after marking in north-western NSW.' *Aust. Mamm.* Vol. 15, June, p.141.

Caughley, G., Brown, B., Dostine, P. & Grice, D., (1984) 'The Grey Kangaroo Overlap Zone.' *Aust. Wildl. Res.* Vol 11

Clancy, T. F. & Croft, D. B. (1990) 'Home range of the Common Wallaroo, *Macropus robustus erubescens,* in far western New South Wales.' *Aust. Wildl. Res.* Vol. 17 (6) pp.659–73.

Close, R. L. & Bell, J. N. (1990) 'Age estimation of pouch young of the Allied Rock-wallaby (*Petrogale assimilis*) in captivity.' *Aust. Wildl. Res.* Vol. 17 (4) pp.359–67.

Coulson, G. (1989) 'The effect of drought on road mortality of macropods.' *Aust. Wildl. Res.* Vol. 16 (1) pp.79–83.

* Dawson, T. J. (1995) *Kangaroos: Biology of the Largest Marsupials.* University of New South Wales Press, Sydney.

Delaney, R. & De'ath, G. (1990) 'Age estimation and growth rates of captive and wild pouch young of *Petrogale assimilis.' Aust. Wildl. Res.* Vol. 17 (5) pp.491–9.

Denny, M. J. S. (1980) Red Kangaroo aris zone studies. Final Report to the Australian National Parks and Wilslife service, Canberra (unpublished)

Domico, T. (1993) *Kangaroos—The Marvellous Mob.* Facts on File Inc. New York.

Ealey, E. H. M. (1967) 'Ecology Euro. Age and growth.' *CSIRO Wildl. Res.,* Vol. 12, pp.67–80.

Evans, M. (1996) 'Home ranges and movement schedules of sympatric Bridled Nailtail and Black-striped Wallabies.' *Wildl. Res.* Vol. 23 (5) pp.547–56.

Finnie, E. P. (1982) 'Husbandry of large macropods at Taronga Zoo, Sydney.' In Evans, D. D. ed. *The Management of Australian Mammals in Captivity.* Proceedings of the Scientific Meeting of the Australian Mammal Society, Healesville, Victoria. February 1979. pp.100–1.

Frith, H. J., and Calaby, J. H. (1969) *Kangaroos.* F.W. Cheshire, Melbourne.

Gemmell, R. T. & Rose, W. H. 'The senses involved in movement of some newborn Macropodoidea and other marsupials from cloaca to pouch.' In Grigg, G., Jarman, P. & Hume, I. *Kangaroos, Wallabies and Rat-kangaroos.* Vol. 1 (1989) pp.339–47 Surrey Beatty & Sons, Sydney.

George, G. G. (1979) 'Tree-kangaroos *Dendrolagus* spp.: their management in captivity.' In Evans, D. D. ed. *The Management of Australian Mammals in Captivity.* Proceedings of the Scientific Meeting of the Australian Mammal Society, Healesville, Victoria. February 1979. pp.102–7.

Green, B. 'Water and energy turnover in free-living macropodoids.' In Grigg, G., Jarman, P. & Hume, I. *Kangaroos, Wallabies and Rat-kangaroos.* Vol. 1 (1989) pp.223–9 Surrey Beatty & Sons, Sydney.

* Hand, Suzanne J. ed. (1990) *Care and Handling of Australian Native Animals. Emergency Care and Captive Management.* Surrey Beatty & Sons, Sydney.

Horsup, A. (1994) 'Home range of the Allied Rock-wallaby, *Petrogale assimilis.' Wildl. Res.* Vol. 21 (1) pp.65-84.

Ingleby, S. (1991) 'Distribution and status of the Spectacled Hare-wallaby, *Lagorchestes conspicillatus.' Wildl. Res.* Vol. 18 (5) pp.501–19.

Insects of Australia. (1970) Sponsored by Div. of Entomology, CSIRO, Canberra. Melbourne University Press.

Jarman, P. & Wright, S. M. (1993) 'Macropod studies at Wallaby Creek. IX*. Exposure and responses of Eastern Grey Kangaroos to dingoes.' *Wildl. Res.* Vol. 20 (6) pp.833–43.

Johnson, C. N. (1987) 'Macropod studies at Wallaby Creek. IV. Home range and movements of the Red-necked Wallaby.' *Aust. Wildl. Res.* Vol. 14 (2) pp.125–32.

Johnson, P. M. (1978) 'Studies of Macropodidae in Queensland, 9. Reproduction of the Rufous Rat-kangaroo (*Aeoprymnus rufescens*) (Gray) in captivity with age estimation of pouch young.' *Qld J. of Agric. & Animal Sciences* Vol. 35 (1) pp.69–72

Johnson, P. M. (1979) 'Reproduction of the plain rock-wallaby *Petrogale penicillata inorta* Gould, in captivity, with estimation of the pouch young.' *Aust. Wildl. Res.* Vol. 6

Johnson, P. M. (1993) 'Reproduction of the Spectacled Hare-wallaby, *Lagorchestes conspicillatus* Gould (Marsupialia: Macropodidae), in captivity, with age estimation of the pouch young.' *Wildl. Res.* Vol. 20 (1) pp.97–101.

Johnson, P. M. & Vernes, K. (1994) 'Reproduction in the Red-legged Pademelon *Thylogale stigmatica* Gould (Marsupialia:Macropodidae), and age estimation and development of pouch young.' *Wildl. Res.* Vol. 21 (5) pp.553–8.

Kirkpatrick, T. H. (1985) 'Biology for management' In Lavery, H. J. (ed.) *The Kangaroo Keepers*. University of Queensland Press, Brisbane.

Kirkpatrick, T. H. & Johnson, P. M. (1969) 'Agile age estimation and reproduction,' *Qld J. of Agric. & Animal Sciences* Vol. 26, pp.691–698

Lee, A. K. & Ward, S. J. 'Life histories of Macropodoid marsupials.' In Grigg, G., Jarman, P. & Hume, I. *Kangaroos, Wallabies and Rat-kangaroos.* Vol. 1 (1989) pp.105–15. Surrey Beatty & Sons, Sydney.

Lundie-Jenkins, G. (1993) 'Reproduction and growth to sexual maturity in the Rufous Hare-wallaby, *Lagorchestes hirsutus* Gould (Macropodidae:Marsupialia) in captivity.' *Aust. Mamm.* Vol. 16 (1) August, pp.45–9.

* McBarron, E. J. (1983) *Poisonous Plants. Handbook for Farmers and Graziers*. Dept. of Agriculture NSW, Inkata Press, Sydney.

McCarron, H. C. K. & Dawson, T. J. 'Thermal relations of Macropodidae in hot environments.' In Grigg, G., Jarman, P. & Hume, I. *Kangaroos, Wallabies and Rat-kangaroos.* Vol. 1, pp.255–63. (1989) Surrey Beatty & Sons, Sydney.

McLean, I. G. & Lundie-Jenkins, G. (1993) 'Copulation

and associated behaviour in the Rufous Hare-wallaby *Lagorchestes hirsutus.*' *Aust. Mamm.* Vol. 16 (1) August, pp.77–80.

Macoboy, S. (1969) *What Flower is That?* Paul Hamlyn, Sydney.

Maynes, G. M. (1972) 'Parma Wallaby.' *Aust. J. Zool.* Vol. 41, pp.107–18.

Merchant, J. C. (1989) 'Lactation in macropodoid marsupials.' In Grigg, G., Jarman, P. & Hume, I. *Kangaroos, Wallabies and Rat-kangaroos.* Vol. 1, pp.355–66, Surrey Beatty & Sons, Sydney.

Merchant, J. C. & Calaby, J. H. (1980) 'Reproductive biology of the Red-necked Wallaby (*Macropus rufogriseus banksianus*) and Bennett's Wallaby (*M. r. rufogriseus*) in captivity.' *J. Zool.*, Lond. 1981, pp.203–17.

* Morris, I. (1996) *Kakadu National Park—Australia.* Steve Parish Publishing.

Murphy, C. R. & Smith, J. R. (1970) 'Age determination of pouch young and juvenile Kangaroo Is. Wallabies,' *Trans. R. Soc. Sth Aust.* No. 94, pp.15–20.

* Murray, Eva (1989) *Living with Wildlife*. Reed Books, Sydney.

Nelson, J. E. & Goldstone, A. (1986) 'Reproduction in *Peradorcas concinna* (Marsupialia:Macropodidae).' *Aust. Wildl. Res.* Vol. 13 (4) pp.501–5.

Poole, W. E., Carpenter, S. M. & Wood, J. T. (1982a) 'Growth of grey kangaroos and the reliability of age determination from body measurements, I. The Eastern Grey Kangaroo, *Macropus giganteus.*' *Aust. Wildl. Res.* Vol 9 (1), pp.9–20.

Poole, W. E., Carpenter, S. M. & Wood, J. T. (1982b) 'Growth of Grey Kangaroos and the reliability of age determination from body measurements, II. The Western Grey Kangaroo, *Macropus fuliginosus fuliginosus, M.f. melanops and M..f. ocydromus.*' *Aust. Wildl. Res.* Vol. 9 (2), pp.203–2.

Poole, W. E., Merchant, J. C., Carpenter, S. M. & Calaby, J. H. (1985) 'Reproduction, growth and age determination in the Yellow-footed Rock-wallaby *Petrogale xanthopus* Gray, in captivity.' *Aust. Wildl. Res.* Vol. 12 (2) pp.127–36.

Poole, W. E. & Merchant, J. C. (1987) 'Reproduction in captive Wallaroos: the Eastern Wallaroo, *Macropus robustus robustus*, the Euro, *Macropus robustus erubescens*, and the Antilopine Wallaroo, *Macropus antilopinus.*' *Aust. Wildl. Res.* Vol. 14 (3) pp.225–42.

Poole, W. E., Brown, G. D. & Inns, R. W. 'Further records of life-spans of the Tammar Wallaby, *Macropus eugenii*

(Marsupialia: Macropodidae), on Kangaroo Island, South Australia.' *Aust. Mamm.* Vol. 11, Nos 1 & 2, June, pp. 165–9.

Priddel, D. (1986) 'The diurnal and seasonal patterns of grazing of the Red Kangaroo, *Macropus rufus*, and the Western Grey Kangaroo, *Macropus fuliginosus.*' *Aust. Wildl. Res.* Vol. 13 (2) pp.113–20.

Priddel, D., Shepherd, N. & Ellis, M. (1988) 'Homing by the Red Kangaroo, *Macropus rufus* (Marsupialia:Macropodidae).' *Aust. Mamm.* Vol. 11, Nos 1 & 2, June, pp.171–2.

Priddel, D., Wellard, G. & Shepherd, N. (1988) 'Movements of sympatric Red Kangaroos *Macropus rufus* and Western Grey Kangaroos *Macropus fuliginosus* in Western New South Wales.' *Aust. Wildl. Res.* Vol. 15 (3) pp.339–46.

* Proske, U. (1996) 'Hopping mad.' *Nature Australia.* Spring. Aust. Museum.

Robertson, G. (1986) 'Mortality in drought—Red Kangaroos.' *Aust. Wildl. Res. Vol.* Vol. 13 (3) pp.349–54.

Robinson, A. C., Lim, L. Canty, P. D., Jenkins, R. B. & Macdonald, C. A. (1994) 'Studies of the Yellow-footed Rock-wallaby, *Petrogale xanthopus* Gray (Marsupialia: Macropodidae), population studies at Middle Gorge, South Australia.' *Wildl. Res.* Vol. 21 (4) pp.473–81.

Rose, R. W. (1989) 'Age estimation of the Tasmanian Bettong (*Bettongia gaimardi*) (Marsupialia:Potoroidae).' *Aust. Wildl. Res.* Vol. 16 (3) pp.251–61.

Rose, R. W. & McCartney, D. J. (1982) 'Growth of the Red-bellied Pademelon, *Thylogale billardierii*, and age estimation of pouch young.' *Aust. Wild. Res.* Vol. 9 (1), pp.33–8.

Russell, E. M. (1972) 'The biology of kangaroos (Marsupialia:Macropodidae).' *Mammal Rev.* 1974, Vol. 4, Nos 1 & 2, pp.1–59.

Russell, E. M. & Nicholls, D. G. (1972) 'Drinking behaviour in the Red Kangaroo (*Megaleia rufa*) and the Euro (*Macropus robustus*).' *Sonderdruck aus Z. f. Saugetierkunde Bd.* H.5, S. pp.311–5.

Sadlier, R. M. F. S., (1963) 'Age estimation by measurement of joeys of the Euro *Macropus robustus* (Gould) in Western Australia.' *Aust. J. Zool.* Vol. 11, pp.241–9.

Seebeck, J. H. (1992) 'Breeding, growth and development of captive *Potorous longipes* (Marsupialia:Potoroidae); and a comparison with *P. tridactylus.*' *Aust. Mamm.* Vol. 15, June, pp.37–45.

Sharman, G. B. & Calaby, J. H. (1964) 'Reproductive behaviour in the Red Kangaroo, *Megaleia rufa*, in captivity.' *CSIRO Wildl. Res.* Vol. 9, pp.58–85.

Sharman, G. B., Frith, H. J. & Calaby, J. H. (1964) 'Growth of the pouch young, tooth eruption and age determination in the Red Kangaroo, *Megaleia rufa.*' *CSIRO Wildl. Res.* Vol. 9, pp.20–9.

Shield, J. W. & Woolley, P. (1961) 'Age estimation by measurement of pouch young of the Quokka (*Setonix brachyurus*).' *Aust. J. Zool.* Vol. 9, pp.14–23.

Short, J. & Turner, B. (1993) 'The Distribution and Abundance of the Burrowing Bettong (Marsupialia: Macropodidae).' *Wildl. Res.* Vol. 20 (4) pp.525–34.

* Smith, Barbara (1995) *Caring for Possums.* Kangaroo Press, Sydney.

Southwell, C. J. (1981) Sociobiology of the Eastern Grey Kangaroo, *Macropus giganteus.* PhD Thesis, University of New England, Armidale.

* Strahan, R. (1981) *A Dictionary of Australian Mammal Names.* Angus & Robertson, Sydney.

* Strahan, R. ed. (1995) *The Mammals of Australia.* Reed Books, Sydney.

Taylor, R. J. & Rose, R. W. (1987) 'Comparison of growth of pouch young of the Tasmanian Bettong, *Bettongia gaimardi*, in captivity and in the wild.' *Aust. Wildl. Res.* Vol. 14, (3) pp.257–62.

Taylor, R. J. (1993) 'Home range, nest use and activity of the Tasmanian Bettong, *Bettongia gaimardi.*' *Wildl. Res.* 20 (1) pp.87–95.

Tyndale-Biscoe, H. (1973) *Life of Marsupials— Contemporary Biology.* Edward Arnold, London.

Walker, D. M. & Vickery, K. (1989) 'Nitrogen balance studies on pouch young *Macropus rufus* and *Macropus giganteus* (Marsupialia:Macropodidae): the utilisation of cow's milk and carbohydrate-free milk replacers.' *Aust. Mamm.* Vol. 12, Nos 1 & 2, June, pp.23–30.

* Walraven, E. (1990) *Taronga Zoo's Guide to the Care of Urban Wildlife.* Allen & Unwin, Sydney.

Walton, D. W. and Richardson, B. J. eds. (1989) *The Fauna of Australia. Vol. 1 B. Mammalia.* AGPS, Canberra.

Wright, S. M. (1993) 'Observations of the behaviour of male Eastern Grey Kangaroos when attacked by dingoes.' *Wildl. Res.* Vol. 20 (6) pp.845–50.

Glossary

ANTIBODY a protein produced in the body of a vertebrate in response to the presence of a foreign substance, which neutralises that substance

AMNIOTIC SAC the sac in which the foetus is born, which breaks immediately after birth

BINOCULAR VISION allows a full three-dimensional image, the clearest form of vision

BLASTOCYST hollow ball of foetal cells with no differentiation of organs

BROWSE to feed on bushes and shrubs

CARNIVOROUS meat eating

CLOACA single cavity into which the excretory, urinary and reproductive tubes open

CYST hollow growth containing liquid

DIURNAL active only during the day

DEFECATE the action of an animal removing wastes from the body; to pass faeces out of the body

ECTOPARASITES surface parasites living on the fur or skin of an animal

EMBRYO living animal in early stage of development before emergence from an egg

EXUDATE something that is exuded, e.g. gum or resin exuding from trees

FOLIVORE leaf-eating animal

FOETUS the young of an animal still in the womb or at the latest stage in an egg

FORB small herb-like plant, not a grass

FORM nest or depression dug under bushes, etc. for resting or sleeping in

GRAZE to feed on grasses and herbs

GREEN PICK fresh green grasses

GREGARIOUS living in groups

GUT FLORA harmless microbes in the gut which aid in the digestion of food

HERBIVOROUS eating vegetation of all types

INSECTIVOROUS eating insects and arthropods

MONOCULAR VISION seeing only movement and a fuzzy image from non-integrated visual images; seeing with one eye

NOCTURNAL active only at night

OESTROUS that time when a female is ready to mate (in dogs called 'on heat' or 'in season')

OOCYSTS female germ cells in the mature stage (of internal parasites)

PENTAPEDAL MOVEMENT—using forelimbs, hindlimbs and tail for locomotion (*pent* = five)

PLACENTAL embryonic development occurring totally in the uterus (not in a pouch)

PREHENSILE/SEMI-PREHENSILE able to grip or partly grip with

PROTOZOAL pertaining to microscopic, single-celled organisms

QUIESCENT BLASTOCYST an early embryo which has temporarily ceased to develop

RANGE/DISTRIBUTION general area which a species is known to inhabit

RHYTHMIC GAIT regular hopping motion (of macropods)

SCLEROPHYLLOUS of plants with tough leaves; there are two forest types—wet sclerophyll and dry sclerophyll, usually having closed canopies

SUBCUTANEOUS just under the skin

TERRITORY an area of habitat occupied and defended by an animal/group of animals

THERMOREGULATION being able to regulate the body temperature

THYLACINE largest marsupial predator in Australia when Europeans first arrived

TUBER thickened underground root

UROGENITAL OPENING external opening into which both urinary and reproductive tracts empty

Index